A Postcard Journey Along the
Upper Mississippi

Robert Stumm

Robert Stumm (signature)

Templegate Publishers
Springfield, Illinois

Copyright © 1997 by Robert Stumm

First published in the United States by
Templegate Publishers
302 East Adams Street
Post Office Box 5152
Springfield, Illinois 62705
217-522-3353
www.templegate.com

ISBN 0-87243-235-1
Library of Congress Catalog Card Number:
97-6093

This book was manufactured in the United States

Introduction

Imagine for a moment you could take a leap backward in time. It is 1907 and you find yourself standing in a swirl of activity waiting to board a steamboat at the St. Paul, Minnesota river landing. Resounding in the fresh morning air are the hurry-up shouts of the boat's crew in a mad struggle to get the last supplies on board. Amidst the bedlam your mind remains focused on the journey that awaits you. Every fiber inside you is alive with anticipation because you are about to experience one of the world's great journeys—a trip down the fabled and storied Mississippi River. You have heard and read about this great river artery all your life but now at last you have the thrill and opportunity to experience it first hand.

Our traveler's journey will be confined to the Upper Mississippi with Cairo, Illinois just under 900 miles from St. Paul, the final destination. The journey awaiting this eager traveler is a slow leisurely passage down a corridor bracketed by majestic bluffs, verdant farmland, and sloughs populated by an ever changing array of migratory birds. This voyage will be a little different from the typical trip because it will include frequent stops at nearly every town along the way. We can presume that this traveler already knows that this or any river is more than just a body of water, but the collective history of the people who live and work along its banks.

What I have endeavored to do with this book is recreate through the use of period postcards what the 1907 traveler would have seen and experienced on a downriver voyage to Cairo. The question that begs to be answered is why did I decide to use postcards to document what the Upper Mississippi River Valley was like in the early years of this century? I think if you understand what it is that made the postcards of that era unique then you'll appreciate why I'm such a fervent believer in their ability to recapture the spirit of a bygone era.

Although postcards had been around from some time, the picture postcard was first introduced in the United States in 1903, and almost overnight they took the country by storm. People were so enamored with them that they used them for exchanging messages with friends in the same town, keeping in touch with a relative in some distant state, or simply collecting them as a pleasant hobby.

To satisfy an almost insatiable demand, postcard publishers documented in an unprecedented way seemingly everything that existed in a town or locality. No subject was considered too mundane so it wasn't unusual to see a watertower or even a nondescript railroad bridge gracing the front side of a postcard. The really compelling aspect to the cards from that era is that they also provide a visual record chronicling how people lived out their lives. Thus if you're lucky enough to locate them it is possible to find cards showing men and women working at a job that no longer exists, gathering together for a public ceremony, or engaged in some type of leisure activity. And, from the perspective of someone interested in the Mississippi River, what really makes these old cards so valuable is that they enable us to look back in time and see how those who lived during that epoch interacted with the river.

What is so astonishing is the variety of postcards emanating from the towns along the Upper Mississippi at the beginning of this century. Consider for a moment that in mid-size communities like Dubuque, Iowa and Galena, Illinois well in excess of 100 different postcards were issued, and even in a smaller town like Keithsburg, Illinois you might find several dozen different cards for sale on a postcard rack. One can only speculate why this area produced such a disproportionately large number of cards but my hunch is that there were two factors at play. The most obvious answer is that it was a manifestation of the number of people traveling along this corridor because in that era postcards were the modern equivalent of today's travel brochure. They provided an opportunity for a town to trumpet everything it valued dear from its parks to its central business district. And I think also, postcards were a barometer of a town's economic vibrancy, and despite whatever woes that might be facing the typical river town, they were far better off than most midwestern communities.

With so many postcards to choose from, selecting which cards to use in this book was a demanding and frustrating ordeal. In the last analysis my main criteria was what were the things that would have caught the eye and imagination of our 1907 traveler. We're trying to capture a moment in time, of course, but what makes this such a vivid experience is that with but a few exceptions, most of the major landmarks and attractions are still around today. Other than the steamboats which worked the river about the only things that haven't survived are the plants and factories which fell victim to a changing economic tide. Therefore, this book can stand and be used as both a history and travelogue.

Although I haven't in any way slighted the great and grand port cities of St. Louis and St. Paul, I have devoted most of my attention and emphasis to the small towns which line the banks of this river. You could say I'm an ardent supporter of the notion that the character and complexion of the Upper Mississippi is mirrored in its smaller towns.

I have singled out and given special attention to three very remarkable towns: Galena, Illinois, Ste. Genevieve, Missouri and Nauvoo, Illinois. Each has a unique and long heritage above and beyond the typical river town. What makes them also deserving of special consideration is that each of them also possesses a magnificently preserved historic district. I think once you've experienced it then you will understand why I have such a fondness for these communities.

You will notice immediately that I took the liberty of including several Minneapolis cards. I did this for several very important reasons. First and foremost, dating way back to the early Nineteenth Century the Falls of St. Anthony was the end point for nearly every river excursion, despite the arduous journey from St. Paul, because it was such a celebrated attraction. In addition, the stretch of river between St. Paul and Minneapolis contains a number of nationally significant landmarks most notably Fort Snelling and the Sibley House.

Unfortunately, and I wish it could have been otherwise, I wasn't able to include a postcard view of every single Upper Mississippi river town. This in no way should be considered a slight on my part. Much of this omission was a matter of circumstance because in the case of many towns there simply weren't any cards of acceptable quality produced in that era. Also, I was constrained by the limits imposed on any writer.

I have tried to encapsulate as much information as possible in the written descriptions that accompany each postcard. When deciding what to write my first thought was always what kinds of insights would readers like to have as they contemplate each scene. Given this imperative information, I tried to give a historic background of each thing under consideration, discuss how it evolved over time and finally provide an update of its current status. My ultimate hope and conviction is that the text will serve as a motivator to get the reader to visit the towns and attractions documented in this book.

In putting together this book I utilized a wide range of research sources. Whenever possible I tried to place the most reliance on contemporary sources of information that ran from county histories to local newspaper stories and accounts. My secondary sources include everything from recent town histories to an assortment of books and articles about the Mississippi River. And needless to say, personal observation played a big role because I've traveled up and down this river more times than I can count.

Finally I'd like to express my thanks and gratitude to all the people who helped make this book a reality. To all the librarians from Hastings to Cairo who were always willing to lend a hand and supply me with whatever information I needed. Also, I was aided by a whole host of people up and down the river who shared with me their personal recollections and remembrances. I am especially indebted to two people: Kate O'Keefe who guided me in the early stages of this project and Kathy Jereczek who somehow managed to make sense of my writing, and for her support and encouragement.

Well we've already kept the other passengers waiting too long so let's get on that boat and head downriver to Cairo.

Robert Stumm

A parenthesis after the card number in the text indicates that a full-color reproduction of the card appears in the insert beginning on page 110. The number identifies the page of the color reproduction and the letter following its position on the page, u for upper and l for lower.

1 (110 u)
St. Anthony Falls

The one true falls on the Mississippi River, St. Anthony Falls provided the interest which gave birth to the City of Minneapolis. Father Louis Hennepin, the Franciscan friar-explorer, was the first European to visit this waterfall in 1680 and named it in honor of St. Anthony of Padua, a patron of his order. Beginning in 1823 the falls became the featured attraction for sightseers touring the river on steamboats. St. Anthony Falls became a permanent power source when the first commercial sawmill was built alongside it in 1847, and two decades later this cataract was powering dozens of mills. Much of the falls' beauty was lost when a wooden apron was placed over it in 1869 to prevent its dissolution into a rapids. The zenith for the falls was the half century from 1880 to 1930 when it provided the waterpower for the city's great flour milling empire. Changes in technology gradually diminished its commercial appeal and today the only thing it powers is a small generating station. Still a source of wonderment, St. Anthony Falls is situated just downstream from the Third Avenue Bridge.

2 (110 l)
West Side Milling District

Hugging the west bank of St. Anthony Falls, this congested ring of buildings was the West Side Milling District, the main hub of Minneapolis' once famous flour milling corridor. When this section of the riverfront was first developed in the 1850's sawmills dominated the landscape, but by 1880 it had been transformed into one long unbroken line of flour mills. They squeezed out other industries because during these years their millers developed a new technology for processing spring wheat, which made Minneapolis flour the best and most profitable in North America. When this photo was taken in 1905 there were 23 mills operating along a narrow one-mile corridor. Responding to a radically altered market environment, mill owners began shifting their operations to other areas of the country in 1930 and the district's lone surviving mill produced its last flour in 1965.

Of the buildings in the scene only a handful have survived. Two have been transformed into office buildings and, incredible as it may seem, one of the old mills is now an elegant four-star hotel.

FALLS ST. ANTHONY MINNEAPOLIS MINN

FLOUR MILLING DISTRICT, MINNEAPOLIS, MINN

3 (111 u)
Stone Arch Bridge

Spanning the river just below St. Anthony Falls, the Stone Arch Bridge was Minneapolis' signature landmark for nearly five decades. The impetus to build this structure arose out of a need to connect Minneapolis by rail to eastern markets. In 1880 James J. Hill, the great railroad financier, agreed to tackle the challenge of building a bridge near the foot of St. Anthony Falls. Many doubted the feasibility of Hill's plan and the project was soon dubbed "Jim Hill's Folly." Hill made them eat crow because the bridge, which was completed in 1883, was a masterpiece of architectural design and planning. Resembling an ancient Roman aqueduct, this stone structure, which makes a sweeping curve across the river, has 23 arches and is just over 2,000 feet in length. After nearly a century of use, the bridge was deactivated by the Burlington Northern Railroad in 1978. Just over a decade later they sold the bridge to the City of Minneapolis, which in the early 1990's converted its deck into a pedestrian walkway. This famous bridge, which provides an unexcelled view of St. Anthony Falls and the adjoining lock and dam, is situated at the foot of Portland Avenue.

4
University of Minnesota

This is a 1903 view of the University of Minnesota, the first university to have the Mississippi River at its doorstep. When the school was chartered in 1851 it was hoped that locating it near the river would be an added inducement to attract students. The whole idea became moot because the school overspent on its first building and that coupled with the Panic of 1857 forced it into receivership. After existing on paper for nearly two decades building began again in 1869 thanks primarily to milling magnate John Pillsbury. Over the next three decades the University blossomed into a first rate institution. For some reason school officials were reluctant to build any structures along the edge of the river and in 1910 they decided to build their new centerpiece mall several blocks to the east of the river. Squeezed for space, the University began expanding along the opposite west bank of the river in the 1960's, and it broke with tradition by erecting buildings with a view of the river. Remarkably, despite all future growth and expansion, with one exception, all of the structures pictured on this postcard are still standing.

The Stone arch bridge and West side milling District, Minneapolis, Minn.

UNIVERSITY OF MINNESOTA. General View.

5
Bohemian Flats

The homes in the foreground of this photo view, taken from the west end of the old Washington Avenue Bridge, were part of a unique river enclave neighborhood called the Bohemian Flats. Situated at the bottom of a steep ledge along a section of the river directly opposite from the University of Minnesota, the Bohemian Flats was populated by first generation European immigrants who, because of their circumstance, needed an inexpensive place to live. Initially occupied in the 1870's, Minneapolis residents called it the Bohemian Flats because a majority of its early residents were Czechs. For those who resided here the river was both a friend and foe. Both young and old alike added to the family income by collecting driftwood, but flooding was almost a yearly spring ritual.

In the 1920's the Bohemian Flats was demolished so the city could build a municipal freight terminal on this site. Today this once isolated area is now a scenic parkway.

6
Riverside Drive

This beguiling scene captures the essence of what has made Riverside Drive the Upper Mississippi's most venerated river boulevard. Straddling the edge of a 100-foot bluff along both the east and west bank of the river between the University of Minnesota and Fort Snelling, Riverside Drive was the brainchild of Horace W.S. Cleveland, the noted landscape architect. Emphasizing the importance of the river, he convinced Minneapolis and St. Paul in the late 1880's to co-develop this 12-mile long route into a parkway. By 1900 Cleveland's dream had become a reality and almost immediately the land adjoining this boulevard became one of the area's most prized residential districts.

Riverside Drive has retained its unspoiled character and over the last three decades it has become one of Minnesota's most popular recreational trails. It's hardly a well-kept secret that in the fall when the leaves are at their peak the parkway is one of America's most beautiful drives.

4288. High Railroad Bridge across Mississippi River, Minneapolis, Minn.

113 Riverside Drive and Lake Street Bridge, Minneapolis, Minn.

7 (111 1)
Minnehaha Falls

This view captures all the tantalizing beauty of Minnehaha Falls, one of this region's oldest and most revered tourist attractions. The first Europeans to visit these falls were soldiers from nearby Fort Snelling and word of their beauty quickly spread downriver. This became a must stop for excursionists touring the river who endured a long and arduous inland pilgrimage from the St. Paul levee to pay homage to this waterfall. Originally called Brown's Falls, in honor of an early settler who ventured to the source of this cataract, they acquired their more lyrical name in the 1840's. Minnehaha Falls were given national exposure when they were so eloquently described by Henry Wadsworth Longfellow in his 1855 poem The Song of Hiawatha. The poem further enhanced the falls' tourist appeal and in an effort to accommodate sightseers Minneapolis developed the land adjoining the falls into a park in the 1890's.

Minnehaha Falls still captures the imagination of sightseers and it is perhaps the most photographed landmark in Minnesota. This much beloved attraction is situated near the junction of Minnehaha Parkway and Hiawatha Avenue.

8
John H. Stevens House

This unpretentious frame structure, was the first house built in the City of Minneapolis. Hoping to establish a town, John H. Stevens built this farmhouse near the west bank of St. Anthony Falls in 1850. Two years later his dream became a reality and the Stevens House became the unofficial town hall and the cultural hub for the new community of Minneapolis. Over the succeeding decades, this once prominent house faded into obscurity until it was rediscovered several miles from its original location by a Minneapolis reporter in 1888. A campaign was launched to restore the house which culminated in one of the most memorable days in the history of Minneapolis. On May 28, 1896, 10,000 jubilant schoolchildren working in relays and aided by a team of horses towed the Stevens House to its new home in Minnehaha Park.

Early in this century the Stevens House was one of the city's most popular attractions but gradually it succumbed to neglect and in the 1940's it was boarded up and all but abandoned. This historic structure was restored at great expense and reopened as a museum in the mid-1980's. Surrounded by a grove of trees, the Stevens House is situated at the south end of Minnehaha Park.

MINNEHAHA FALLS MINNEAPOLIS, MINN.

THE STEVENS HOUSE, (FIRST HOUSE BUILT IN MINNEAPOLIS, MINNEHAHA PARK, MINNEAPOLIS, MINN.

9
Fort Snelling

This woman is gazing across the river at Fort Snelling, which in a real sense was the birthplace of Minnesota. The northernmost fort on the Mississippi River, Fort Snelling was established on a high bluff overlooking the mouth of the Minnesota River in 1819 and completed six years later and named in honor of its first commander, Colonel Josiah Snelling. Over the next three decades it served as a gathering point for fur traders and settlers and helped plant the seed from which grew St. Paul in 1840 and Minneapolis just over a decade later. In the 1850's the fort was converted into a supply depot and by the end of the century most of its original stone buildings had been torn down and replaced. This historic fort was finally deactivated by the Army in 1946 and handed over to the Veterans Administration.

In the early 1960's the Minnesota Historical Society began rebuilding the original fort. The process consumed almost two decades and this complex of over a dozen meticulously restored buildings ranks among the country's finest historic sites. Part of a 2,500 acre state park, Fort Snelling is situated just north of the Minneapolis St. Paul International Airport.

10
Sibley House

We are looking at a side view of the oldest surviving dwelling in the State of Minnesota. In 1834 Henry Sibley, a young fur trader, arrived at Fort Snelling and one year later built this two-story stone house on a bluff overlooking the mouth of the Minnesota River. His home became the nucleus for the village of Mendota and he assumed the role of the region's most influential settler. Sibley was selected as a representative to Congress in 1849, and nine years later he became Minnesota's first elected Governor.

Sibley and his family moved from Mendota to St. Paul in 1862 and over the next four decades the structure was everything, from a school, to a railroad warehouse, before it was finally abandoned around 1900. In 1909 the Daughters of the American Revolution purchased the Sibley House and restored it as a museum to its original condition. This museum is furnished with period items and a number of Sibley family heirlooms. Often called the Mount Vernon of Minnesota, this historic structure is situated near the junction of Highway 13 and the Mendota Bridge.

FORT SNELLING-MISSISSIPPI AND MINNESOTA RIVERS, ST. PAUL, MINN.

4264. Sibley Home, Oldest Building in State, now owned by the D. A. R., Mendota, Minn.

11
High Bridge

One can easily see from this river perspective why this towering metal structure was called the High Bridge. The High Bridge had a unique status because it was the Upper Mississippi's one and only legitimate bluff-top to bluff-top bridge. Completed in 1889, it connected St. Paul's heretofore isolated Upper West Side with the east bank of the river. Nearly 200 feet above the river at its highest point, its deck was locked in place by 25 dry land piers. The bridge passed the ultimate design test when it survived a direct blow by a monstrous tornado in 1904.

In the late 1970's this aging structure was declared unsafe and it was razed in 1985. Just before the High Bridge was demolished a group of local residents honored its passing by staging an elaborate mock funeral. A concrete bridge built in 1987 now spans this section of the river but it lacks the mesmerizing appeal of its much beloved Nineteenth Century predecessor.

12
Lower Landing

Taken from the Robert Street Bridge and looking downriver, this scene captures the last waning days of St. Paul's storied Lower Landing, which shaped and defined the character of this great river city. The initial group of settlers who founded St. Paul in the early 1840's coalesced around this point on the riverfront because it was situated at the foot of a natural opening, a steep 80-foot ledge. Residents called it the Lower Landing because there was a second landing a mile upstream which was quickly superseded in importance by this river terminal. By 1850 the Lower Landing had become the true head of navigation on the Mississippi thereby enabling St. Paul to assume its longstanding role as the region's leading distribution center. Over the next two decades the landing was also the main point of entry for the great army of European immigrants who migrated to Minnesota. St. Paul became essentially a railroad town in the 1870's and by 1905 when this picture was taken the Lower Landing had regressed to the status of a terminal for excursion boats.

Time has obliterated all trace of this once famous river landing which was located at the end of Jackson Street. None of the buildings in this picture have survived and unfortunately the land adjoining the river is now a four lane highway.

HIGH BRIDGE, ST. PAUL, MINN.

River Scene in St. Paul.

13
Indian Mounds Park

This glorious panoramic view showcases the earthen mounds of Indian Mounds Park, Minnesota's most conspicuous ancient burial site. Archaeologists tell us that the prehistoric people who inhabited the Mississippi Valley even before the time of Christ believed that bluff tops were sanctified ground. At these sacred places they conducted religious ceremonies and buried their dead in conical mounds. One of the best examples of this phenomenon is Dayton's Bluff, the hill on which these mounds are located. When European settlers arrived here in the 1830's they found several dozen mounds on this bluff, the majority of which were quickly destroyed. Fortunately, the few remaining mounds were excavated by a succession of archaeologists between 1856 and 1883 and thanks to their work we now know these earthen mounds were built by people of diverse cultures spanning a period from approximately 500 B.C. to 1500 A.D.

Prompted in large measure by these excavations St. Paul decided to preserve the last six surviving mounds and in 1893 created Indian Mounds Park. This beautifully landscaped park is located about two miles south of downtown St. Paul at the junction of Earl Street and Mounds Boulevard.

14
St. Paul Union Stockyards

These horses are waiting to enter an auction barn on the outer edge of the St. Paul Union Stockyard which in its heyday was one of the largest stockyards in the world. This facility was established in 1886 by a group of investors led by Alpheus Stickney on a large undeveloped tract of land adjoining the west bank of the river just south of St. Paul. One year later the town of South St. Paul sprang up alongside this fledgling complex. In its early years this was a transfer point for hogs and cattle until 1897 when Swift and Company arrived here and built a large packing plant and slaughterhouse. Soon other packing companies were attracted here to this stockyard and by World War I it had grown into a daunting complex of barns, pens, and processing plants. The peak period for this livestock facility occurred in the 1950's when almost 10,000 people were employed here. In an effort to economize, packing companies like Swift began pulling out of this stockyard in the 1960's and within two decades nearly all activity had ceased at this facility. Although the livestock industry still has a small presence here it has largely been transformed into an industrial park which is bounded on the east by a very scenic trail.

THE INDIAN MOUNDS, ST. PAUL, MINN.

Horse and Mule Company Barns, South St. Paul

15 (112 u)
Spiral Bridge

North America's one and only spiral bridge, this fanciful structure was Hastings, Minnesota's most treasured landmark for nearly six decades. Hastings residents had lobbied long and hard for a bridge to connect them with the east bank of the river and in 1895 their dream was finally realized. Who designed this 360-degree spiral is still a matter of conjecture, but its purpose was to funnel traffic directly into the town's commercial district. The bridge became an instantaneous attraction and people drove miles out of their way just to ride across this unique structure. It was a perilous journey in inclement weather but the townspeople of Hastings cherished this bridge because it gave them something to boast about.

Load restrictions were placed on this structure in the 1930's and a decade later the state decided to build a new highway bridge 100 feet upstream from the Spiral Bridge. Hastings tried valiantly to preserve this time-honored bridge but the effort failed and it was razed in 1951. Even after what is now almost half a century the people of Hastings still cherish the memory of this unique bridge.

16 (112 l)
Dakota County Courthouse

The Dakota County Courthouse is one of the oldest and most attractive government buildings in the State of Minnesota. In 1857 the county seat was moved from Mendota to Hastings and for nearly a decade the county offices were housed in the second floor of a malting company. Action on a courthouse was delayed by the Civil War and then finally in 1867 the county hired the state's foremost architect, A.M. Radcliff, to design this highly decorative structure, which was completed in 1871. Built of salmon colored brick, the building is a blending of various architectural styles, but what clearly sets it apart are its four corner towers which are crowned by curved mansard roofs. The ornate Renaissance dome was added to the structure in 1912.

Dakota County built a new government center west of Hastings in the mid-1970's and there was talk in the air that this building might be torn down. Cooler heads prevailed and the county spent a great deal of money restoring the courthouse in the late 1980's. In 1991 Hastings purchased this structure and subsequently converted it into the city hall. This beautiful building is located on a hill at Third and Vermillion.

SPIRAL BRIDGE, HASTINGS, MINN.

Dakota County Court House, Hastings, Minn.

17 (113 u)
Vermillion Falls

This charming waterfall is Hastings' own mini-version of St. Anthony Falls. In 1853 Harrison Graham settled in Hastings and built a small mill on the north bank of this cataract on the Vermillion River. He sold some of Minnesota's first flour but was unable to turn a profit, and in 1863 Stephen Gardner purchased the mill. Gardner built a new multi-story milling complex equipping it with the latest technology, and he quickly became one of the state's most successful mill owners. The Gardner family owned the mill until late in the Nineteenth Century and then it passed through a number of hands before it was purchased by the Peavy Company in 1924. They initiated a massive building program and this complex, which is now owned by Con Agra, is one of the world's largest flour mills.

In the 1970's Hastings built a small park running along the south bank of the Vermillion Falls at the corner of 21st and Vermillion. The park's main attraction is a viewing platform that offers up a wonderful close-up perspective of this waterfall and a section of the original Gardner Mill.

18
Prescott, Wisconsin

Here is a bird's eye perspective of Prescott, Wisconsin. The photo was taken from the west bank of the St. Croix River. Named for Philander Prescott, a soldier and fur trader who built a cabin on this site in 1839, Prescott is located at the confluence of the St. Croix and Mississippi Rivers. Originally called Elizabeth, it was founded in 1851 and quickly became an important transfer point for freight. Cargo moving up the Mississippi destined for towns along the St. Croix River was unloaded at this junction and then transferred into vessels that plied the St. Croix. When the steamboat era ended Prescott's economy collapsed and the town became a sleepy backwater.

Over the last three decades this once tiny village has become a boomtown. Prescott's reemergence from obscurity was ignited by the scenic appeal of the St. Croix Valley. Viewed from this same perspective today, the biggest change has occurred along the Prescott riverfront, for it is now home to a thriving marina.

Vermillion Falls, Hastings, Minn.

Bird's-Eye View of Prescott, Wis.

19 (113 l)
Red Wing

For sheer beauty its hard to imagine a more captivating scene than this view of Red Wing, Minnesota in a photo taken from an upriver island. Positioned on the river just above the head of Lake Pepin, Red Wing was initially settled in 1851. Almost overnight this new town became one of the state's principal wheat markets and just two decades after its establishment Red Wing had over 4,000 residents. Red Wing's dependence on the river ended in the 1880's when it became a major center for the production of earthenware pottery. Its two large pottery companies, which eventually merged in 1906 into the Red Wing Stoneware Company, were nationally recognized for their fine jars and crock pots. In the 1920's the company shifted its emphasis to dinnerware and after years of declining sales and a protracted labor battle it went out of business in 1967.

Red Wing is still primarily a manufacturing center but it also has a strong tourist component to its economy. In addition to its scenery, the town's biggest draw is its diverse selection of historic architecture.

20
Christ Episcopal Church

Christ Episcopal Church is one of Red Wing's most prominent public landmarks. This church was organized in 1858 by Reverend Edward Wells, a native New Yorker who was just starting his career in the ministry. One year later under his direction, the congregation built a handsome frame church. They quickly outgrew this structure and after a brief fund-raising drive work commenced on this edifice in 1869. The church, which cost just over $25,000, was completed in the fall of 1871. Its very compact steeple was added to the frame in 1897.

Great care has been taken to preserve this structure, which has been remodeled several times in this century. Built of limestone chiseled from Barn's Bluff, the church has Gothic style pointed arch windows and a most impressive gable entry. Christ Episcopal Church is situated at the foot of a small park at the corner of West Third Street and East Avenue.

Red Wing from Wisconsin Shore

Christ Church, Red Wing, Minn.

21 (114 u)
Barn's Bluff

I have taken the liberty of including this 1929 view of Barn's Bluff even though it falls outside the parameter of this book because it documents the Kiwanis Steps, the first stairway to climb all the way up a Mississippi River bluff. Red Wing literally grew up around the base of this bluff and the residents of this community shared a common desire to ascend this 330 foot high hill. However reaching the summit had never been easy, which is why in 1889 C.W. Webster organized a group of volunteers to carve out a path up the west face of the bluff. The trail, which became known as Webster's Way, made the hill more accessible but it was difficult to maintain and it was eventually abandoned. In the 1920's the local Kiwanis Club devised a creative plan to build a concrete stairway up this bluff. To finance the project they sold individual steps to the public and the purchaser got to have his or her name inscribed on the step. Completed in 1929 the stairway quickly became Red Wing's most popular tourist attraction.

In 1959 this stairway was dismantled to accommodate a new highway bridge. Most of the steps were saved and in the 1970's several segments of the old stairway were rebuilt on the southeast face of the bluff. This stairway is situated at the foot of East Fifth Street.

22 (114 l)
Lake Pepin

We are looking upstream, in this blufftop view, at Lake Pepin, the one section of this great river that has all the characteristics of an actual lake. Named for an Eighteenth Century fur trader, Lake Pepin is a 30 mile long widening of the river extending from just below Red Wing, Minnesota to Reeds Landing, Minnesota. It was created approximately 10,000 years ago by a natural dam at the mouth of the Chippewa River. The Europeans who settled this region in the mid-Nineteenth Century quickly became enamored with Lake Pepin and over the course of time it has been one of the most popular boating and fishing venues in the upper midwest.

There is also an unpleasant side to this very beguiling body of water. Rivermen live in fear of this lake because they know a storm can whip it into a raging cauldron capable of destroying any boat. The most tragic incident on these waters occurred on July 13, 1890 when the Sea Wing, a steamer loaded with over 200 excursionists, encountered a sudden storm near Maiden Rock, Wisconsin. Violently thrown about, the boat capsized and in the ensuing chaos 98 lives were lost.

BARN'S BLUFF, SHOWING STAIRWAY, RED WING, MINN.

"ON THE CHICAGO, MILWAUKEE & ST. PAUL RAILWAY"

23
Maiden Rock

Towering high above the waters of Lake Pepin, this rock-faced bluff is Maiden Rock, where in an age-old Dakota legend a young princess plunged to her death. In this tragic tale, a beautiful maiden named Winona falls madly in love with a young brave from a different tribe. Following the tribal tradition, her parents dissolved the relationship and arranged a marriage to an older brave whom Winona didn't love. Heartbroken, she slipped away from the village and climbed to the summit of this bluff where she ended her life.

Near the base of Maiden Rock is a historic marker commemorating this centuries-old Indian story. This celebrated landmark is located four miles south of Maiden Rock, Wisconsin.

24
Frontenac Inn

In 1900 this massive structure was the Upper Mississippi Valley's most elegant resort hotel. The origins of this hotel date back to 1857 when Israel Garrard, a wealthy Kentucky lawyer, decided to establish a genteel resort community on the shores of Lake Pepin. After housing guests in his home for nearly a decade, Garrard decided to build a hotel that would cater to the upper crust of society. Completed in 1867, the Lakeside Hotel drew nationwide attention to Garrard's little community of Frontenac. Capable of accommodating 150 guests, the hotel had its own ballroom, boathouse, a billiard room and ladies parlor and adjoining it was a racetrack where visitors could train their horses. While it catered primarily to rich southerners one of the hotel's most notable guests was General Ulysses S. Grant.

Shortly after Garrard died in 1901 the hotel was purchased by a local resident who renamed it the Frontenac Inn. From 1939 to the mid-1980's the hotel was part of a Methodist youth camp. Located at the north end of what is now called Old Frontenac, this hotel is currently being utilized as a corporate retreat.

MAIDEN ROCK NEAR LAKE CITY, MINN.

A953 FRONTENAC INN - SIDE VIEW - FRONTENAC, MINN.

33

25
Lake City, Minnesota

This postcard features a fountain and Lake City, Minnesota's City Hall. It was taken from the center of what is now Patton Park. Situated near the mid-point of Lake Pepin, Lake City was platted as a town in 1855. Lake City started out as a grain port but almost from its very inception this community became a haven for vacationers drawn here by the awesome beauty of Lake Pepin. As river traffic declined, tourism gradually took on an even greater role in this town's economy, and then in the first two decades of this century, Lake City was a major button manufacturing center. In the summer of 1922 when Ralph Samuelson, a local resident, invented the sport of water skiing.

Other than Lake Pepin, Patton Park is this city's most compelling attraction. Most of this community's major buildings, including City Hall built in 1899, are grouped around this delightful old town square, whose centerpiece is still this rustic stone fountain.

26
Camp Lakeview

In what almost looks like a vignette from the Civil War, this scene shows a group of Minnesota national guardsmen firing artillery during a drill at Camp Lakeview. Established in 1905 on the outskirts of Lake City, Minnesota, Camp Lakeview was the summer training base for the state's National Guard. Because it was laid out along the river, the camp became an irregular stop for excursion boats who were gladly welcomed, except of course when live ammunition was being fired. One can imagine also that being on the river relieved some of the drudgery associated with military training.

Because it needed more space to conduct maneuvers, the guard abandoned Camp Lakeview for a site up in northern Minnesota in 1930. Time has erased nearly all traces of the camp and most of the land it occupied has been swallowed up by Lake City.

Oaklyn Park and City Hall, Lake City, Minn.

ARTILLERY AT CAMP LAKEVIEW, LAKE CITY, MINN.

M-28 ILLUSTRATED POST CARD CO., N. Y.

Pub. by F. H. Phillips

27
Reed's Landing

Nearly the entire community of Reed's Landing, Minnesota is captured in this view taken from a bluff looking downstream. Located directly opposite form the mouth of the Chippewa River near the southern tip of Lake Pepin, Reed's Landing was founded in 1847 by a Canadian named Charles Reed's. Starting out as a shipping point for grain, it rapidly evolved into one of the river's most notorious rafting towns. Rafts which had been pushed through Lake Pepin were boarded at this juncture by the hard-living crewmen who steered them downriver. Reed's Landing became filled with saloons and brothels where lawlessness was a way of life. With vice as its main industry this community became little more then a ghost town when the rafting era ended.

Reed's Landing is now one of the smallest communities in Minnesota and only a handful of the buildings in this scene have survived. The town's most notable survivor is the large building at the far right, an 1870 schoolhouse which has been converted into a county museum.

28
Pepin, Wisconsin

A lot of time and effort must have been invested in taking this photographic view of Pepin, Wisconsin from the end of a stone pier. Situated just downstream from Lake City, Minnesota, Pepin was platted as a town in 1849 by William Newcomb. Unlike most river towns, Pepin lacked a natural harbor and as a consequence it never developed into a commercial center, and in its early years it was little more than a cluster of buildings. By the end of the nineteenth Century, Pepin had grown into a modest farming village, and over the last several decades it has blossomed into a very popular tourist destination. This community is also associated with Laura Ingalls Wilder, the noted children's writer, who was born just east of here in 1867.

Extending out into the river about 50 yards, this pier was built in the 1890's to create a marina. A path now runs down the center of this pier, which has become a popular viewing platform.

29
Wabasha

Wabasha, Minnesota's Main Street, was still a dirt thoroughfare when this photo was taken in 1905. Located just downstream from the foot of Lake Pepin, Wabasha was initially settled in 1843 and platted as a town in 1854. Originally called Cratte's Landing, it was renamed in honor of a Nineteenth Century Dakota Sioux Indian Chief. For nearly two decades Wabasha was one of the state's leading wheat markets and in the 1880's its riverfront was home to a small boat building yard. The town retained its vitality through the waning days of the steamboat primarily because it was a county seat.

Possessing a fine complement of two-and three-story commercial buildings, downtown Wabasha has changed very little over the course of the last century. Most of these structures were built between 1870 and 1890 and great care has been taken to preserve their original character.

30
Wabasha Boat Livery

The simple pleasures of a bygone era are wonderfully expressed in this view of a boat livery at Wabasha, Minnesota. Once a common fixture in river communities like Wabasha, a boat livery had an assortment of pleasure craft which one could rent for a fishing outing or a leisurely jaunt on the river. Usually they were owned and operated either by a retired pilot or someone who worked at the local boatyard who needed some extra spending money. Notice that several of the boats have outboard motors which were just starting to come into vogue, and needless to say they would one day completely revolutionize water recreation.

Boat liveries, which provided an economically risky livelihood. As the Twentieth Century progressed, more and more people became boat owners and the marina displaced the boat livery.

Main Street, Wabasha, Minn.

BOAT LIVERY, WABASHA, MINN.

31
Alma, Wisconsin

Mother Nature had obviously deposited a fresh blanket of snow on Alma, Wisconsin in this bone-chilling mid-winter scene. Alma, on the shore of the river about midway between Lake City and Winona, Minnesota, was initially settled in 1848 by two Swiss immigrants, Victor Probst and John Waecker, and five years later it was incorporated as a town. Like so many of the other river towns of this region, Alma first rose to prominence as a shipping center for wheat. Historically this community is most often associated with the Beef Slough, a log rafting complex located two miles upstream near the mouth of the Buffalo River. Established in 1867 on a backwater channel, the Beef Slough was where logs which had been floated down the Buffalo River were processed and assembled into rafts. When it was abandoned in 1890 Alma suffered a sharp and severe economic reversal.

Wedged in a narrow corridor between the bluffs and the Mississippi, Alma is now a charming New England Style resort community. Outwardly it has changed very little since 1900 and in the late 1980's the entire town was placed on the National Register of Historic Places.

32
Fountain City

Taken from a bluff this all encompassing panoramic photo captures both the river and nearly all of Fountain City, Wisconsin. Situated eight miles upstream from Winona, Minnesota, Fountain City was first settled in 1839 by Thomas Holmes who made a living here by selling cordwood to steamboats. Colonized by German immigrants, the town became the agricultural market for the southern half of Buffalo County. Later a lumbering center, Fountain City received a much needed shot in the arm when the Corps of Engineers decided to establish a service base along its levee in 1894. This boatyard which is still in operation serves as the Corps' primary repair and storage facility for its St. Paul District.

Viewed from this same perspective today, Fountain City looks much like it did in 1900. The only fundamental change has occurred along its riverfront which has been cleared of all its old mills and warehouses and is now home to a marina.

Main St., Alma Wis.

33 (115 u)
Levee Park

Taken from a bridge deck looking south, this card provides a panoramic view of Winona, Minnesota's Levee Park. Laid out in 1896, the park was the first conscious and deliberate effort on the Upper Mississippi to create an aesthetically pleasing riverfront. The city fathers of Winona developed this beautifully landscaped park so its citizenry could enjoy the Mississippi and convey as well a favorable image of the town for those traveling on the river. Crisscrossed with paths, Levee Park was essentially the prototype for the modern riverfront park which catered to walkers.

Sadly, Winona has gone in the opposite direction from nearly every other Upper Mississippi community. The grass and paths have disappeared and a large section of this century old park is now a parking lot. Situated at the foot of Main Street, the park's featured attraction today is a replicated version of an old steamboat.

34
Winona County Courthouse

The Winona County Courthouse is one of Minnesota's premier examples of late Nineteenth Century public architecture. Work on this structure, which was designed by a local architect, was initiated in the summer of 1888, and the courthouse was dedicated just over a year later on September 16, 1889. Built of brown sandstone and featuring a large arched entryway and ornamented with an array of towers and turrets, this edifice was a fine example of Richardsonian Romanesque Architecture.

In 1958 county officials, caught up in the spirit of urban renewal, began an intense campaign for a new courthouse. Opposed by a small but vocal group of preservationists, they attempted and failed three times to win voter approval to replace this structure and finally, in desperation, they conceived a plan to build it without a bonding referendum. This elicited such a negative reaction that finally in 1971 the board capitulated and $1.65 million was appropriated to remodel this grand old building. Now one of the city's most cherished landmarks, the Winona County Courthouse is located at the corner of Washington and Fourth Street.

2905. Levee Park, Winona, Minn.

Court House, Winona, Minnesota.

35
Winona State University

This mammoth structure housed for many years the entire campus of what is now Winona State University, Minnesota's first public teachers' college. The City of Winona was so delighted at the prospect of having what was then called a normal school that it built a two-story multi-purpose structure for this institution, which opened in 1860. Enrollment expanded rapidly and in 1865 the state appropriated funding for this building, which was completed in 1869. Educators of that era believed that containing everything under one roof made for a better learning atmosphere, so in addition to housing the school's classrooms and administrative offices the building had a library, museum, an assembly hall and a separate dormitory wing. As the school grew they just kept adding to the frame of this edifice and the campus didn't expand one building until 1903.

In the first two decades of the Twentieth Century several new buildings were added to the campus and the timing couldn't have been better because this structure, which the students called Old Main, burned to the ground on December 3, 1922. Winona State University, which is located on the western edge of downtown Winona, now has over two dozen buildings on its campus.

36
St. Stanislaus Catholic Church

St. Stanislaus Catholic Church stands as a monument to the Polish immigrants who settled Winona in the Nineteenth Century. Lured by the prospect of a better life, a large contingent of Poles migrated to Winona in the 1860's. Occupying an enclave at the south end of town, they decided in 1871 to form their own parish, which they named in honor of St. Stanislaus Kostka. They built a small frame church, which they quickly outgrew, and then moved into a somewhat larger stone edifice. Having grown into one of the largest parishes in the diocese, they laid the cornerstone for this ornate structure in 1891, and the church was completed in 1894.

Combining elements of Baroque and Romanesque styling, St. Stanislaus is one of the most intricately designed churches in the midwest. Executed in beautiful red brick, the church has an octagonal frame which is surmounted by a neo-classic dome. The sanctuary, which seats 1,800, is lavishly decorated with stone carvings and metal grille work. This architectural gem with its Old World charm is located at the corner of Fourth and Carimona.

WINONA, MINN.   NORMAL SCHOOL
Made exp. for Jno. T. Faber, Milwaukee, Wis.

Greetings from
Winona to Madonna
F.

St. Stanislaus Church and School, WINONA,
S'w. Stanislawa Kościół i Srkola.

37
Sugar Loaf Bluff

The stone-capped hill in this idyllic scene is Sugar Loaf Bluff, one of this river valley's most distinctive landmarks. Prior to European settlement this bluff, which sits in the southwest corner of Winona had a different name and appearance. Indians of this region called it Wapasha's Cap because its summit resembled a red cap worn by Chief Wapasha who wintered with his tribe at the base of this structure. The bluff had a rounded shaped summit until two Irish brothers, John and Stephen O'Dea, started quarrying rock here in 1878. Displeased because they felt the O'Dea's were disfiguring this landmark, Winona residents finally convinced them to abandon their operation in 1887. However, as a result of the quarrying the summit was now surmounted by a stone knob and almost immediately it was re-nicknamed Sugar Loaf Bluff.

Over time Sugar Loaf became Winona's most significant landmark and in 1950 it was purchased by the Daughters of the American Revolution who then deeded it to the city. Once a reference point for riverboat pilots, this bluff is situated at the junction of Highways 61 and 43.

38 (115 l)
Ice Skating - Winona

Looking at this scene of youngsters skating on the river at Winona reminds us that children, unlike most adults, appreciate and embrace winter. In this era children relished the opportunity to frolic and play on the frozen waters of the Mississippi. Once it was clear the ice was thick enough they would shovel away the snow and create their own private rink. They wore bulky wooden skates, which in no way deterred them from often skating from sunrise to sunset. Occasionally when the temperature was a little milder, some of the bigger kids would go on a skating expedition to the next town on the river.

One can only wax nostalgic for this once joyous wintertime ritual. Skating, except within the confines of an indoor rink, has become passé and the youngster of today, reared on television and video games, would never dream of skating on the Mississippi River.

Winter Sports, Winona, Minn.—28

39
Trempealeau Mountain

Casting a shadow which extends almost to the far bank of the river, this giant monolith is the storied Trempealeau Mountain, the Upper Mississippi's one and only island bluff. This 425-foot high bluff is situated at the mouth of the Trempealeau River, one mile upstream from Trempealeau, Wisconsin. The Sioux, who inhabited this region called it "Minnay Chonkahaha" the "Bluff in the Water." They had a legend that this bluff was carried by a spirit, from its original location near modern day Red Wing, and deposited here during a storm. In reality it was separated from the adjoining bluff thousands of years ago when the river carved out a new channel.

The first European to visit this bluff was Nicholas Perrot who built a trading post at the base of this structure in 1685. In the Nineteenth Century steamboat pilots used the bluff as a navigational landmark. Still a source of wonderment, Trempealeau Mountain is now one of the main attractions in Perrot State Park.

40
Trempealeau Wisconsin

One would be hard pressed to conjure up a more idyllic scene then this view of Trempealeau, Wisconsin, sandwiched between the river and the bluff which the residents here call First Peak. This community's history can be traced back to 1840 when John Reed built a rudimentary cabin where he established what quickly became a very popular inn and tavern. Out of deference to its first settler, this fledgling village was originally known as Reed's Landing, and for a brief period in the 1850's, it was called Montoville, and then in 1856 residents agreed to call it Trempealeau. Thanks to its fine natural harbor, this settlement quickly became a major shipping point for wheat, but after the market for this commodity collapsed in the 1870's, Trempealeau's main attraction was that of a picturesque river village.

Only a few of the buildings and homes shown here are still standing as gradually the population moved away from the river. This movement away from the river has occurred in nearly every community along the Upper Mississippi as residents and businesses redirected their orientation to the railroad line and later to the main arterial highway passing through town.

Trempealeau, Wis., from the River on the Burlington Route.

41 (116 u)
Steamer Quincy

Here the steamer Quincy struggles for survival after hitting a snag near Trempealeau, Wisconsin in the summer of 1906. Snags, which are submerged trees, were the principal risks for steamboats from the earliest days of navigation on this waterway. The Upper Mississippi bristled with snags because of its many islands and the constant erosion of its banks. Unlike boiler explosions or fire, there was nearly always ample time to safely evacuate a boat impaled on a snag.

On this occasion the Quincy was a good deal luckier than most boats. All the passengers and crew scrambled to safety after she ran aground, and then the Quincy was successfully raised and put back into service at the Dubuque boatyard.

42
Heileman Brewing Company

When this picture was taken the G. Heileman Brewing Company had already been in business for over half a century. The great wave of German immigrants who settled along the Upper Mississippi in the years between 1840 and 1880 brought with them a very strong brewing tradition and it wasn't all that uncommon during this period for even a small river community to have two breweries competing against one another for business. Gottlieb Heileman was very much a part of that tradition. He arrived at La Crosse in 1852 and just two years later he and a partner established what would become the Heileman Brewing Company. Over the next three decades his German lager became the city's most popular beer and after surviving prohibition the company repositioned itself as a leading regional brewery.

This facility which is now owned by Stroh's Brewery is situated along the 900 block of South Third Street. Although the brewery has modernized its facilities the two largest buildings in this scene, the brew house and stock house, are still an integral part of this complex.

Steamer Quincy sunk near Trempeleau, Wis.,
on the Mississippi River

G. Heileman Brewing Co., La Crosse, Wis.

43 (116 l)
Swimming Beach at Pettibone Park

The people in this nostalgic scene are frolicking in the water at Pettibone Park, the Upper Mississippi's oldest existing public swimming beach. So much attention has been focused on the Mississippi's unhealthy condition that its hard to conceive of anyone wanting to swim in this river, but back at the beginning of this century practically every Upper Mississippi community had a designated swimming area on the river. Responding to pressure from their health departments, communities began closing these beaches just before World War I and by 1920 only the hardiest of souls were swimming in this river. The first steps taken to clean up this occurred in the 1920's and 1930's when towns stopped dumping untreated sewage into the Mississippi. In the 1960's government agencies started cracking down on corporate polluters and by the late 1970's beaches began springing up along this waterway.

Situated on an island opposite downtown La Crosse, this beach opened in 1904 and the only time it was deemed unsafe to swim here was a several year stretch in late 1930's. This facility looks quite different today because it now has a very large and expansive beach, a picnic area, and a modern concrete boathouse.

44
St. Rose Chapel

The St. Rose Chapel is La Crosse, Wisconsin's most celebrated religious landmark. In 1870 the Franciscan Sisters of Perpetual Adoration decided to move their convent from Jefferson, Wisconsin to La Crosse. They chose La Crosse as their new home because it had a large and growing Catholic community and its leaders hoped that an urban setting would draw more women to their order. The diocese felt it only right and proper that these sisters after a quarter century of tireless dedication should have their own house of worship. The chapel's cornerstone was laid in 1904 and this monumental edifice was completed in 1906.

Designed by Eugene Liebret, a noted Milwaukee architect, St. Rose Chapel is a highly embellished example of Romanesque Revival Architecture. The rich stone exterior is dominated by a series of fortress-like towers. Its stunning sanctuary is decorated with imported statuary and exquisitely crafted stained glass windows. This nationally renowned chapel is located at Ninth and Market.

8326. Public Bath House and Swimming Pool, La Crosse, W

LA CROSSE WIS. ST. ROSE CHAPEL
OF PERPETUAL ADORATION

45 (117 u)
Grandad Bluff

Standing like a giant on the eastern edge of La Crosse, Grandad Bluff is one of this river valley's largest and most conspicuous bluffs. It was given its name because one of its rock outcroppings resembles a human face. The bluff's summit was the site of La Crosse's first formal religious service held on the morning of June 23, 1850. Nineteen years later right in the midst of La Crosse's most extended building boom. J.S. Bantam started quarrying from this massive 525-foot high bluff. And over the next quarter of a century the rock quarried from Grandad was the city's primary source of building material. In 1912 two of the city's wealthiest families, the Hixons and Funks, deeded the bluff to the city so its summit could be developed into a city park.

Now one of La Crosse's most popular attractions, Grandad Bluff has a road which winds all the way up to its summit. The bluff's park, which covers 150 acres, contains a large picnic area and a not-to-be-missed viewing platform.

46
Dredging

The structure on the right in this river scene is the dredge Vulcan operating on an island in the vicinity of La Crosse, Wisconsin. From the 1870's right up to the present day, dredges like the Vulcan have played an essential role in helping maintain an open channel for navigation of the Upper Mississippi. Their assigned task is to clear the river of any debris that might pose a hazard to boats—rocks, snags, silt and, of course, sandbars. Especially in this era, a dredge might spend a month or more working in one location. The Vulcan, which was one of the earliest dredges to work this section of the river, was operated and maintained by the Corps of Engineers at their service base in Fountain City, Wisconsin. In comparing it to its modern counterpart, the biggest difference is that the Vulcan had to be towed from one location to the next.

Grand Dad Bluff,
La Crosse, Wis.

47
Desoto, Wisconsin

This is an advertising card issued by the Burlington Northern Railroad. The panorama showcases the tiny village of DeSoto, Wisconsin. Situated four miles upstream from Lansing, Iowa, DeSoto was platted as a town in 1854 by a group of proprietors led by Dr. James Osgood. Originally called Winneshiek's Landing, it was renamed in honor of Hernado DeSoto, the Spanish explorer who was the first European to actually see the Mississippi River. DeSoto's close proximity to Lansing prevented it from developing into anything more than a river landing of modest size. This village's most prosperous years were the decades between 1860 and 1880 when its riverfront was lined with sawmills.

A quaint fishing village, DeSoto has changed very little over the last century. About the only thing different in this scene today is that a highway now runs through this village.

48 (117 1)
Lansing, Iowa

This superb panoramic is from a bluff at the western edge of Lansing, Iowa. Situated 12 miles downstream from the Iowa-Minnesota border, Lansing was founded in 1851 by John Haney. Emulating the pattern of so many other river communities, Lansing started out as a shipping center for grain and then in the 1870's lumbering became the town's principal business. Lansing entered a new phase in 1897 when J. M. Turner began operating the town's first button factory. By 1900 this community had three button companies and over the next half century it ranked second in the nation behind only Muscatine, Iowa in the quantity of buttons produced.

Lansing, which has seen its population drop by over 25 percent since 1900, is now a service and distribution center. The town's main attraction has always been its spectacular scenery.

Village of De Soto Wis. from bluffs South of Village on the Burlington Route.

Lansing and Mississippi from the Bluffs, Lansing, Iowa.

49
Lynxville, Wisconsin

This bluff top photo of Lynxville, Wisconsin looking north was probably taken around 1904. Positioned on the river 12 miles downstream from Lansing, Iowa, Lynxville was platted as a town in 1857. It was named for a steamboat called the Lynx which plied this section of the Mississippi River in the mid-Nineteenth Century. Settlement here was less than robust because Lynxville was established fairly late and in its early years this village was primarily a fishing and fish processing center. Lynxville enjoyed its greatest prosperity in the period between 1870 and 1890 when it was an assembly point for log rafts headed downriver.

A village struggling simply to survive, Lynxville has lost nearly half its population since 1900. From this perspective today Lynxville, which clings to the side of a large bluff, looks much as it did at the end of the Nineteenth Century.

50 (118 u)
Harpers Ferry, Iowa

This panoramic view shows a steam locomotive passing through the town of Harpers Ferry, Iowa. The diminutive river village, which sits just downstream from Lynxville, Wisconsin, was settled in the late 1840's and named as one might expect in honor of a Mr. Harper, who operated a ferry service between here and Lynxville. Its close proximity to a number of prominent river ports hindered its development into a steamboat landing of any consequence and most of its inhabitants eked out a living as commercial fisherman.

Harpers Ferry, like a number of the adjoining river towns in this area, has over the twenty years recast itself into a resort community. While much has changed here the town has managed to preserve its two most treasured landmarks, St. Ann-St. Joseph Catholic Church, the building in the far left corner, and next to it the old town schoolhouse which is now a community center.

No 9
1908
BIRDS EYE VIEW,
LYNXVILLE, WIS.

Birdseye View of Harpers Ferry Iowa.

Prairie du Chien, Wisconsin

This postcard shows the main business district of Prairie du Chien, Wisconsin, a town whose history dates all the way back to the Seventeenth Century. One can trace its beginning to the morning of June 17, 1673 when Father Jacques Marquette and Louis Joliet paddled out of the Wisconsin River and into the Mississippi. Their epic voyage was significant for many reasons, but perhaps most important of all, it established a waterway link between the Great Lakes and the Upper Mississippi, and logic dictated that trading emporiums would spring up at both ends of this route. This first recorded trading activity at the mouth of the Wisconsin River dates to 1686 when Nicholas Perrot built an outpost near the present site of Prairie du Chien.

For the next 60 years there were only sporadic contacts between the French and the Indians of this area until sometime in the 1750's when they began meeting regularly each spring and fall on a broad plain which French traders called "Le Chien" in honor of a Fox Chief. Around 1770 a small settlement started to form at this site. It was little more than a ragtag group of cabins strung out along the riverfront. Late in the Eighteenth Century some of the wealthier traders began building homes, but Prairie du Chien didn't take on the appearance of a real town until 1816 when a contingent of American soldiers arrived at this village and built Fort Crawford.

Thanks mainly to the ingenuity and drive of Hercules Dousman, Prairie du Chien became a major shipping port for furs and pelts destined for eastern markets. And by 1840, this once isolated trading outpost had become a thriving commercial center. It was, however, still largely a one-industry town, and when the fur market declined in the 1840's, Prairie du Chien was rapidly superseded in importance by its upstream neighbor, La Crosse. But over the years Prairie du Chien has become a manufacturing center and a favorite summer tourist vacation spot.

Bluff Street was Blackhawk Avenue several decades ago, and has retained most of its Nineteenth Century buildings. However, like most midwestern towns, most of this community's economic activity has shifted to its outlying highway corridor.

BLUFF STREET, LOOKING WEST, PRAIRIE DU CHIEN, WIS.

52
Villa Louis

Nearly enveloped by trees in this view, the Villa Louis is one of this river valley's most illustrious house museums. This mansion is part of the legacy of Hercules Dousman, who arrived at Prairie du Chien in 1826 as an agent for the American Fur Company. Through his various endeavors, Dousman amassed a great fortune and in 1843 he built an elegant brick home atop a large Indian mound. Dousman died in 1868 and two years later his widow razed their home and erected a posh Victorian style mansion. Her son and his wife lived in the Villa Louis until the 1890's and then it was used primarily as a summer retreat by the Dousman family. In 1935 the Dousman family deeded the home to the city of Prairie du Chien and seventeen years later the State Historical Society of Wisconsin assumed ownership of this magnificent edifice.

Architecturally the most notable feature of the Villa Louis is the glassed-in porch which encircles two-thirds of the building. It is furnished with museum-quality items including a Steinway Grand Piano, several hand-carved beds, an exquisite china set, and a small church altar. Recognized as one of the midwest's finest Victorian mansions, this structure is located at 521 North Villa Louis Road.

53
Fort Crawford

This deteriorating stone building was the last surviving vestige of Fort Crawford, which played a pivotal role in the early history of Prairie du Chien. In 1814 a contingent of soldiers arrived at this trading outpost and built Fort Shelby, which was captured almost immediately by the British, who burned it to the ground in 1815. A year later the U.S. Army built a second fort here naming it in honor of the then Secretary of War, William H. Crawford. Fort Crawford ended British influence in the area and enabled Prairie du Chien to develop into a real town. The fort was badly damaged by a series of floods and in 1829 the army built a new fort on higher ground, which was occupied the following winter. By the 1840's the fort had fulfilled its initial mission and it was formally abandoned in 1856.

In the years that followed all of the fort's structures were dismantled and used for building material with the exception of its hospital, shown here in this 1900 photograph. This historic landmark was rebuilt by the Federal Government in 1934 and it now houses the Fort Crawford Medical Museum. One of Prairie du Chien's most popular attractions, this museum is located at the junction of Rice and South Main Street.

4037   VILLA LOUIS   PRAIRIE DU CHIEN, WIS

Ruins of Fort Crawford, Prairie du Chien, Wis.

54
St. Gabriel's Church

St. Gabriel's Catholic Church is Prairie du Chien's oldest and most important public landmark. This parish was founded in 1832 by Father Samuel Mazzuchelli. After worshipping for eight years in a modest structure, parishioners launched a drive to build a new church which was completed in the summer of 1842. Father Mazzuchelli designed this stone church and personally supervised much of its construction. It was subsequently enlarged. The church's most distinctive feature is its rounded arch ceiling. The building's side towers were added to the frame in the latter part of the Nineteenth Century.

For over a century, St. Gabriel's has been closely associated with its most beloved priest, Father Lucien Galtier, who served this parish from 1847 until his death in 1866. Despite his long years of service, Galtier is best remembered for establishing the first church at St. Paul in 1841 and changing the city's name from Pig's Eye to St. Paul. Forgoing the usual practice of burying remains under the altar, St. Gabriel's decided to build his crypt near the church's main entrance, and if you look closely you can see his tomb at the right edge of its landscaped terrace. St. Gabriel's is located at 506 North Beaumont.

55
Log Raft

Taken in the waning last days of log-rafting on the Upper Mississippi, this extraordinary panoramic view shows a steamer skillfully maneuvering an enormous raft past a railroad bridge at Marquette, Iowa. In the initial phase of this long and colorful epoch, which began in the 1840's, rafts were floated downriver and steered to their destination by a crew of oarsmen. The raft itself was formed by inserting staples at the end of each log and lashing them together to form sections, which were then bonded together to create these multi-block long behemoths. Steamboats were first used to push rafts downriver in 1863, but it took two decades to displace the rafting crews because of the limited number of steamers with the capability to carry out this difficult assignment.

In the years from 1900 to 1910, what was once an unending procession of rafts was reduced to a few lonely stragglers. Finally in 1915 they became part of the river's lore when the last raft was pushed downriver from Hudson, Wisconsin to Fort Madison, Iowa.

ST. GABRIEL'S CHURCH, PRAIRIE DU CHIEN, WIS.

Rafting on the Mississippi. Passing through Pontoon Bridge, Marquette, Iowa

51099-N

56
Marquette, Iowa

We are looking directly down from a bluff at the old North McGregor railroad yard. On the opposite bank from Prairie due Chien, Wisconsin, North McGregor started developing into a river community in the late 1840's. Hardly more than an appendage of its downstream neighbor McGregor, Iowa, this village never evolved into anything more than a minor riverboat landing. It finally took on a life of its own late in the Nineteenth Century when it became a division point on the Chicago, Milwaukee, and St. Paul Railroad. The most lasting and immediate impact of the railroad's presence was the establishment of several new large hotels.

In the early years of this century the town changed its name to Marquette in honor of Father Jacques Marquette who explored this great river in the summer of 1673. All vestiges of the town's railroad yard have been wiped away by the passage of time and Marquette exists today as a quiet village which becomes slightly more animated during the summer tourist season.

57
McGregor, Iowa

We are looking down the Main Street of McGregor, Iowa in this glorious bluff top panorama. Positioned on the river two miles downstream from Prairie du Chien, Wisconsin, McGregor was founded in 1847 by Alexander McGregor, a very successful ferry boat operator. The town's early growth was nothing short of spectacular. Within a decade of its founding, McGregor had grown into one of the busiest wheat ports on the Mississippi River and by the mid-1860's its population had swollen to over 4,000 and it had well in excess of a hundred businesses. McGregor never managed to diversify and when the wheat market collapsed in the mid-1870's its economy was thrown into a state of upheaval. When things finally stabilized this community had repositioned itself into a service and distribution center and at the end of the Nineteenth Century it had almost 1,500 inhabitants.

Nicknamed the "Pocket City" because it sits in a natural amphitheater, modern McGregor is now a year-round tourist destination. Much of its appeal results from its preservation of so much of its Nineteenth Century architectural heritage.

VIEW AT NORTH McGREGOR LOOKING SOUTH ON MISSISSIPPI RIVER.

A 247   Pocket City, McGregor, Iowa.

58 (118 1)
Lewis Hotel

A throwback to a bygone era, this charming McGregor inn, which is now called the Alexander Hotel, has been a source of pride for this community ever since it opened in 1899. It was about twice the size of most small town hotels, a clear indicator that McGregor had already become a fashionable tourist destination. Although first class in every respect, with amenities that included a dining room, barber shop, several private parlors and a bar, an overnight stay here cost only half a dollar in 1900.

Even though the interior has changed considerably over the years, the exterior of the Alexander looks almost exactly as it did when this picture was taken. McGregor's most conspicuous landmark, this fine old hotel is located at 213 Main Street.

59
St. Mary's Catholic Church

St. Mary's Catholic Church symbolizes the strong German Catholic tradition that persists to this day in McGregor. This parish, like most of the Catholic churches in northeastern Iowa, was founded by a missionary from Dubuque in 1857. Soon after its establishment the parish built a beautiful wood frame church. In 1876 the church burned to the ground in a disastrous Christmas Eve fire. With an ever resolute faith, the parish erected this handsome stone church in 1882.

Since 1882 the one really major alteration to the church occurred just a few years ago with the addition of a bell tower. Unpretentious yet still very attractive, St. Mary's Church sits at the base of a bluff on the west end of Main Street.

THE LEWIS HOTEL, MC GREGOR, IOWA.

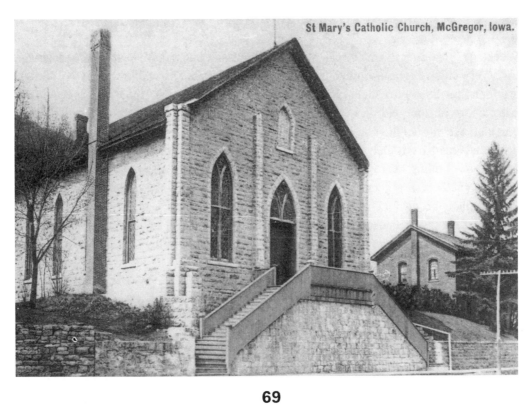

St Mary's Catholic Church, McGregor, Iowa.

60
Pike's Peak

Appearing to float in space, this well dressed gentlemen, who was added to the scene by the postcard publisher, is standing atop Pikes Peak, one of the great natural wonders of this scenic river valley. Strategically positioned directly opposite the mouth of the Wisconsin River, this massive 500 foot bluff was first occupied by members of a mound-building culture sometime around 500 B.C. This towering landmark was one of the first things that the French explorers, Father Jacques Marquette and Louis Joliet, saw when they entered the Mississippi River on the morning of June 17, 1673. Well over a century later in September of 1805, Lieutenant Zebulon Pike made the first formal survey of this bluff and it was subsequently named in his honor.

In the 1930's the State of Iowa purchased this bluff and made it a state park. In addition to possessing one of the river's finest viewing platforms, the park also has a very picturesque waterfall and a small sand cave. One of the most popular camping spots in the midwest, Pike's Peak State Park is situated one mile south of McGregor, Iowa.

61
Clamming

Working their way through a small mountain of mussel shells, these people are searching for a very elusive treasure, the fresh water pearl. The mad scramble for pearls, which are found inside mussel shells, lasted form 1890 to 1920 on the Upper Mississippi and coincided with the peak years of the button industry, because those engaged in this pursuit made most of their money selling discarded shells to button manufacturers. Shells were dislodged from their bed with a tool called a crowfoot dredge. They were then hauled to a boiling tank on the river bank where they were steamed open. Searching through shells was a game of persistence because only one in approximately every 25,000 clams produce a marketable pearl.

The quest for pearls ended in the 1920's primarily as a result of overharvesting. Over the last two decades there has been a mini-resurgence in pearling activity thanks to the conservation efforts of the Federal Government.

E 9782 BREAK O'DAY ON THE MISSISSIPPI, FROM BEAUTIFUL PIKES PEAK, JUST BELOW McGREGOR, IOWA

Looking for the Pearl, the Hidden Treasure.   Scene on the Mississippi.
Near the Tri Cities, North and South McGregor and Prairie Du Chien.

62
Wyalusing, Wisconsin

Unbelievable as it may seem this junkyard of a building was for many decades the commercial and social hub of Wyalusing, Wisconsin. Positioned on the river just downstream from the mouth of the Wisconsin River, Wyalusing was founded in 1856. Although it possessed an ideal river landing this fledgling settlement faced a number of serious handicaps. Access to the interior from here was nearly impossible because of the mountainous terrain and it was located in close proximity to a number of more established river communities. Even at its peak in the 1870's Wyalusing was nothing more than a tiny fishing hamlet and over the course of time it has never had more than two dozen buildings. Wyalusing survives today as a haven for summertime boaters.
Dating from the late Nineteenth Century, the Wyalusing Post Office was the village's general store. It should come as no surprise that this firetrap burned to the ground in 1934.

63
Guttenburg, Iowa

Although it has a rustic look about it, Front Street was the main commercial artery of Guttenburg, Iowa back at the beginning of this century. Situated on the river about midway between Prairie du Chien, Wisconsin and Dubuque, Iowa, Guttenburg was founded in 1845 by a group of German immigrants. They named their community in honor of Johannes Gutenberg, the inventor of movable type, but due to a misunderstanding they misspelled his name. Benefiting from its close proximity to several very profitable lead mines, Guttenburg was settled quickly and by the late 1850's it had nearly 1,000 inhabitants. After its initial spurt the town's population stabilized at that figure over the next three decades and Guttenburg became primarily an agricultural market. The button industry helped reinvigorate the town's economy in the 1890's and was the leading job provider until World War II.
Parallel with Guttenburg's riverfront, Front Street, which is now River Park Drive, has retained much of its Nineteenth Century character. One of the street's most notable buildings is an 1856 warehouse which has been converted into a restaurant.

POST OFFICE
WYALUSING, WIS

Front St., looking South, Guttenberg, Iowa.

64
St. Mary's Catholic Church - Guttenburg

For nearly a century this handsome twin-towered church has been the social and religious hub for the community of Guttenburg. St. Mary's parish, which in its initial years had a strong German identity, was established here in 1851. Built in that same year, the parish's first church was a modest two-story frame building. In 1873 this structure was replaced by a much larger stone edifice. As a result of the growth in membership in the 1890's, in 1901 a consensus was reached to build a new church. Designed by Reverend J.H. Brinkman, the parish' priest, this structure was completed in 1903 at a cost of $29,000.

Built of St. Louis pressed brick with limestone trim, this church has changed very little in the last ninety odd years. An exemplary example of German Romanesque Revival Architecture, this structure's towers rise to a height of 146 feet. Far and away this community's most conspicuous landmark, St. Mary's Catholic Church is located at the corner of Schiller and South Second.

65
Clam Shell Pie - Guttenburg

One has to stare at this card in amazement because, believe it or not, these gentlemen are sitting atop a pile of discarded clam shells that came from one of the button plants at Guttenburg, Iowa. This gives you some idea of the magnitude of the button industry along the Upper Mississippi in the early decades of this century, because there were at one point dozens of plants similar in size to the one in this photograph. The question of course that begs to be answered is how did they dispose of all these shells? Most of the shells were either used for road fill or sold to farmers who ground them down and used them as feed.

If you're at all into scavenging, you should be happy to know that this river valley still has a bountiful supply of old discarded shells. One of the places you might want to start your search is the south end of the Guttenburg riverfront, which is covered with a very conspicuous layer of shells.

St. Mary's Church, Guttenberg, Iowa

66
Cassville, Wisconsin

Except for the three gentlemen at the right, this scene of Cassville, Wisconsin's Main Street is devoid of any life or activity. Positioned on the river eight miles downstream from Guttenburg, Iowa, Cassville was platted as a town in 1836 by a group of New York real estate speculators. They were betting that Cassville would become the territorial capital of Wisconsin and to help sway sentiment in their favor they built a four-story building to house the state legislature. When Madison was chosen instead, Cassville teetered on the brink of extinction. Those who had settled here somehow persevered and Cassville eventually became a fairly important river port.
A community still very much connected to the river, Cassville has one of this area's last car ferries. Main Street hasn't changed all that drastically but isn't nearly as vigorous as it once was.

67
Potosi, Wisconsin

Probably taken from a church steeple, this photo shows the commercial district of Potosi, Wisconsin. Positioned on the river 10 miles upstream from Dubuque, Iowa, Potosi developed around a lead mine discovered here in 1827 by Willis St. John. During its initial two decades Potosi was a major shipping point for lead and one of the largest settlements in Wisconsin. The town's economy suffered a double blow when many of its miners left to join the California Gold Rush of 1848 and when the price of lead declined precipitously in the 1850's. By 1860 this one-time boom town had dropped to the status of a small farming village. Many have come to associate the town with its brewery whose beers were popular in southwestern Wisconsin in the decades between 1880 and prohibition.
Most of the buildings in this scene were destroyed in a series of fires that rocked this community in 1916 and 1919. Despite these losses and its diminutive size, Potosi still possesses an interesting array of historic buildings including a blacksmith shop that dates from 1848.

Main Street, Cassville, Wis.

BIRD'S EYE VIEW, POTOSI, WIS.

68
High School – Potosi, Wisconsin

Whoever took this postcard view of the Potosi High School was obviously having some fun at the expense of the boys in this wintry scene. Built in 1867 this structure, which residents called the "New Brick School," was the town's second public school building. Back in the Nineteenth Century and the early decades of this century simply getting to school was an accomplishment. The only way to get to and from school was by walking, which also meant that if you lived out in the country you had to stay in town with a friend during the school year if you wanted an education.

This building served as the Potosi High School until 1958. Shortly thereafter it was converted into an apartment building. One of the oldest surviving structures in Potosi, it sits atop a small hill at 109 East Street.

68A
The Dubuque Ice Harbor

Here is the Dubuque Ice Harbor in the first decade of this century. Built in 1885 by the Corps of Engineers to provide a winter haven for steamboats, the harbor was the longtime home of the Dubuque Boat and Boiler Works, the Upper Mississippi's premier boat building company. Producing its first boat in 1870, this company initially specialized in building iron-hulled steamboats. Its most famous vessel launched in 1901 was the Sprague, which measured 318 feet in length and was the largest steamboat ever built. In the last years of operation, the boatyard produced primarily small pleasure craft, before it finally went out of business in 1972.

None of the buildings immediately adjacent to the riverfront in this picture have survived, and today this section of the harbor is home to a magnificent set of six museums collectively called "Mississippi River Museum." The oldest museum in this complex is housed inside the building just to the left of the clump of trees, which in this era was a railroad freight depot. This museum and the others adjoining it are located alongside the Third Street overpass.

"HIGH SCHOOL"
POTOSI, WIS.
NO. 10.

take your choice
Maggie.

INNER HARBOR, DUBUQUE, IOWA.

69
Dubuque Harbor

Two partially completed vessels are on display in this view of a portion of the Dubuque, Iowa Harbor. The Iowa Iron Works Company established a yard in 1870 when they started building iron hull boats. Thanks to the company's innovative technology it quickly became the largest boatyard on the Upper Mississippi River. The most famous vessel ever built at the yard was the *Sprague,* a towboat which those on the river called "Big Mama". Launched in 1901, the *Sprague* was 276 feet long, had a 40 by 40 foot paddle wheel and it set a world record in 1907 when it pushed 60 barges loaded with coal.

Around 1950 the yard shifted its focus from building commercial boats to excursion craft. Once the largest inland shipyard in America, the facility was phased out of existence in 1972.

70 (119 u)
Dubuque Shot Tower

The Dubuque Shot Tower stands today as a lone sentinel recalling the days when Dubuque's economy was centered around lead mining. A shot tower was a quick and efficient way to manufacture huge balls of lead called shot. Molten lead was poured through an opening in the top of the tower. As it traveled downward it passed through a series of screens that shaped it into a sphere, ending its journey in a vat of cooling water.

This limestone tower, which rises to a height of 150 feet was built in 1856 by a group of local businessmen. During the Civil War the tower produced well in excess of 1,000 shots per day. Soon after the war ended it was converted into a lumberyard watchtower. In 1911 the tower was abandoned after it was severely damaged in a fire. Fortunately through a joint public-private partnership, the tower was restored in the 1950's to ensure its survival. One of our country's last remaining shot towers, this structure is located at the east end of Fourth Street.

In the Harbor, Dubuque, Iowa.

64566

THE OLD DESERTED SHOT TOWER, DUBUQUE, IOWA.

71 (119 l)
Fenelon Place Elevator

At first glance this looks like an amusement ride, but in reality this Dubuque attraction is the most imaginative solution ever concocted to surmount a river bluff. The idea for what is now called the Fenelon Place Elevator was born out of a desire by J.K. Graves to shorten the commuting time between his home at the top of the bluff and his office downtown. After considering a number of options, Graves contracted with a local engineer to build a cable car, which made its first run on July 25, 1882. It wasn't long before Graves began letting the public use his car and there was a great sense of loss when the cable system burned to the ground in 1893. Within a matter of weeks a group of citizens formed a company which built a new and improved system employing two counterbalancing cars which they opened in the fall of 1893. Remarkably the only major modification to the system occurred in 1977 when the original cars were replaced.

Over the last decade alone over a million people have ridden on the Fenelon Place Elevator. Often billed as the "World's Steepest, Shortest, Scenic Railway," this one of a kind attraction is located at the corner of 4th and Bluff.

72 (120 u)
Majestic Theater

Obviously a building of some distinction, the Majestic Theater was one of the river valley's most splendid pre-World War I theaters. Patterned after a Paris theater, the Majestic was the epitome of elegance when it opened in 1910. Like any good theater, it had an opulent lobby and richly decorated balconies, but what really set it apart was its exterior stonework and its very unusual Mansard roof.

In the 1920's this theater was converted into a movie house and renamed the Orpheum. The building underwent a slow process of decay and by 1960 it was in a sorry state of disrepair. Thankfully, this community recognized its historic value and in the early 1970's it was renovated at great expense and recast into an ultra modern family entertainment complex. A stellar example of historic preservation, this structure, which is now called the Five Flags Theater, is located at Fourth and Main.

MAJESTIC THEATRE, DUBUQUE.

73
Dubuque County Courthouse

The Dubuque County Courthouse is more than just a magnificent work of architecture, or a noteworthy landmark, but the ultimate statement of civic pride. In the 1890's public architecture was a way for cities and municipalities to affirm and proclaim what they had achieved, and with this edifice Dubuque made a resounding declaration that it had become a great city. Monumental in every respect, this building, which was completed in 1893, measures 88 by 125 feet and has a central tower that rockets skyward to a height of 190 feet. One of the features of its design is the multitude of large allegorical figures that grace the exterior.

The Dubuque County Courthouse has retained all of its original grandiloquent styling and as a fitting tribute, it was the first building in Dubuque to be listed on the National Register of Historic Places. Obviously hard to miss, it is located downtown at 720 Central Avenue.

74 (120 l)
St. Raphael's Cathedral

St. Raphael's Cathedral is the one major Dubuque landmark that dates back almost to the very founding of this community. Dubuque was still only a half-civilized mining town in 1850 when Bishop Mathias Loras decided to build a Cathedral here that would last for an eternity. Construction was a painstaking slow process that lasted from 1852 until 1859, and even then there was still work to be done because the 130-foot central tower wasn't added to the frame until 1876.

St. Raphael's still ranks as one of the midwest's finest church buildings, a testimony to the foresight of Bishop Loras. Among the more notable aspects of this Gothic Revival style building are its exquisitely detailed windows and a magnificent set of fresco paintings depicting various saints. A landmark whose historic importance cannot be overstated, this Cathedral is situated at the southwestern edge of downtown at Second and Bluff.

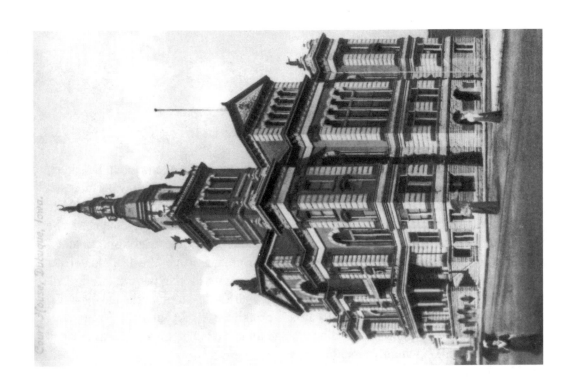

Court House, Dubuque, Iowa.

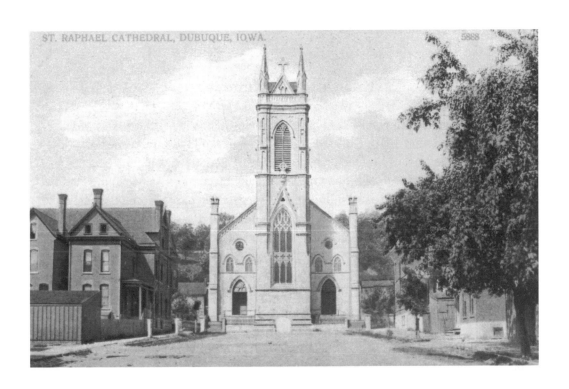

ST. RAPHAEL CATHEDRAL, DUBUQUE, IOWA.

5888

75
Dubuque Monument

This monument stands atop the grave of an extraordinary Frenchmen, Julien Dubuque, the first permanent white settler in what would become the State of Iowa. Dubuque, who was only in his teens, migrated to the settlement of Prairie du Chien in 1785 to trade in furs, but quickly shifted his focus to lead mining. Using his personal charm he was granted a concession in 1788 by the local Fox Indians to extract lead from the mines near the mouth of the Catfish Creep. Once a year Dubuque hauled his lead downriver to St. Louis on a keelboat, and it wasn't long before he was living the life of a French nobleman. He resided in a large house furnished with European imports and even had a small library. Dubuque died in 1810 after a protracted illness, and the Fox Indians paid homage to his memory by building a stone tomb over his grave that was situated on a bluff overlooking the Mississippi River.

Late in the Nineteenth Century the City of Dubuque decided to honor its namesake and in 1897 they dug up his remains and placed them in a new grave just a few feet away, over which they built this 30-foot high tower. Honoring a unique man, the Dubuque Monument is situated at the southeastern tip of Dubuque near the junction of Grandview Avenue and Julien Dubuque Drive.

76
East Dubuque, Illinois

This view looking west down the Main Street of East Dubuque, Illinois was probably taken sometime around 1910. Situated in the extreme northwestern corner of Illinois directly across the river from Dubuque, Iowa, East Dubuque was platted as a town in 1854. Originally called Dunleith, the town essentially owed its existence to the fact that the Illinois Central Railroad started ferrying passengers and cargo from this location to Dubuque in 1855. Dunleith's economy was centered around its role as a transfer point and the town was left badly crippled when the Illinois Central finally built a bridge here in 1868. For better or worse, East Dubuque is usually associated with the many speakeasies it had during the Prohibition days of the 1920's and throughout the midwest it was known as "Sin City."

East Dubuque has pretty much shed its notorious past although it does still have more than its share of nightclubs. The town's Main Street has undergone a dramatic transformation since 1910 but several buildings have survived, most notably the structure at the far right which is now a law office.

TOMB OF JULIEN DUBUQUE, DUBUQUE, IOWA.

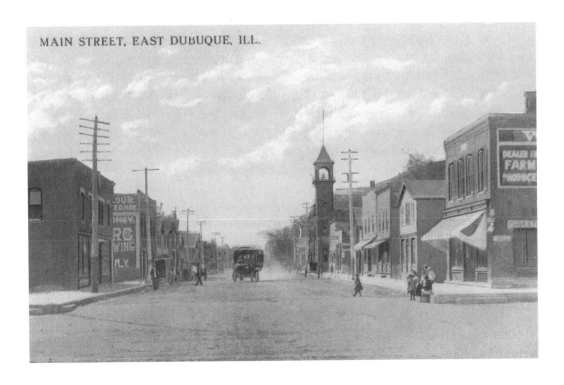

MAIN STREET, EAST DUBUQUE, ILL.

77
Galena, Illinois

Taken from Grant Park, this photo gives a panoramic view of Galena. In 1690 Nicholas Perrot, a French explorer, was the first European to see Indians mining lead in this area. Over the years Galena became a mining settlement. By 1830 it had nearly 1,000 inhabitants. By 1850 Galena was the largest town in Illinois and it was popularly believed that it would one day rival Philadelphia or Cincinnati. But when the Illinois Central Railroad built its bridge at Dubuque, when the price of lead declined sharply and the Galena River channel narrowed the town's fortunes fell.

With the 1960's came a revival and a belated recognition of the town's rich architectural heritage transformed Galena into one of the most attractive tourist destinations in the midwest.

78
U.S. Grant Home

The U.S. Grant Home stands as a tribute and memorial to the man most often associated with Galena, Ulysses S. Grant. What most people aren't aware of is that prior to the Civil War, Grant had lived in Galena for just eight months. That didn't preclude the town from claiming him as their hometown hero, and when he arrived back here on August 18, 1865 they held a grand celebration in his honor. On that day they presented this house, built in 1859, as a gift to Grant and his family with underlying hope that they would make Galena their permanent home. Regrettably, Grant had other plans and he returned here only sporadically using this house as a summer retreat. In 1904 the Grant family deeded the house to Galena and almost immediately it became a hit tourist attraction which, since 1931, has been managed by the State of Illinois.

The U.S. Grant Home, which by any measure is a very modest two-story brick house, takes on a special aura because it is furnished entirely with items that belonged to the Grant family. This famous historic site is situated near the top of a hill at Fourth and Bouthillier.

LOOKING WEST FROM GREENE ST. BRIDGE. GALENA, ILL.

79
Desoto House

Dating all the way back to the days when Galena was still a bustling riverport, the Desoto House is one of the midwest's oldest surviving hotels. Built on the expectation that Galena would become a huge metropolis, the Desoto House was the equal of any big city hotel when it opened in the spring of 1855. A stately five story building, the hotel originally had 225 guest rooms, a reading room, several parlors and a huge elegant dining hall. Over the course of the next two decades it played host to a number of important events, including an 1856 speech by Abraham Lincoln, and in both 1868 and 1872 it served as the campaign headquarters for Ulysses S. Grant. The two upper stories of the hotel were removed in 1880.

In the Twentieth Century the hotel, which was now primarily a boarding house, slowly drifted into disrepair. Fortunately, its historic value was recognized and in the mid-1980's several million dollars were spent revamping it into an elegant modern hotel with just 55 guest rooms. A landmark which in many ways has mirrored the history of Galena, the Desoto House is located at 230 South Main.

80
First Presbyterian Church

A building with a commanding countenance, the First Presbyterian Church is the second oldest surviving church still in use in the Upper Mississippi Valley. First Presbyterian was organized in 1831 by Reverend Aratus Kent, who two years earlier had preached the first sermon in Galena. Starting with just six original members the Congregation expanded at a brisk pace and in 1838 there were able to build this edifice which is styled in the manner of a New England Church. The church's most notable feature, its exquisitely crafted steeple, was added to the frame in 1855.

Embodying the spirit from a time when Galena was just starting to develop into a town, this church is in a remarkable state of preservation. What is really extraordinary is that the church has managed to retain so many of its original appointments. The original pews remain in place. Long one of the most photographed buildings in Galena, the First Presbyterian Church sits on a terrace overlooking the main business district at 106 N. Bench Street.

DeSoto House, Galena, Ill.

First Presbyterian Church, Erected 1838, Galena, Ill.

81
Galena Post Office

Over what is now almost a century and a half, the Galena Post Office has been the one constant in a town that has experienced so much economic upheaval and change. Impressive in every detail, this structure was completed in 1857 at a cost of $61,000, a sum which reflects Galena's prosperity at the time. In its early years, this building also doubled as a custom house where import and export duties were collected.

This post office was never replaced simply because Galena kept shrinking, and in a real sense the building outgrew the town. Constructed of cut limestone, this beautifully designed edifice is one of the most notable structures in Galena. The exterior looks almost exactly as it did in 1857, and although the interior has been modified substantially it has retained a great deal of its original mahogany woodwork. One of the oldest post offices in America, this historic gem, which few tourists ever bother to visit, is located at the intersection of Green and Commerce.

82 (121 u)
Galena Levee

Pondering this tranquil scene of a sleepy levee with only the presence of a few small pleasure craft it seems almost inconceivable that in the years between 1830 and 1850 Galena was one of the busiest inland ports in the United States. Most of the flotilla of steamers that arrived at Galena came to pick up lead for transport downriver and quite a number of the residents here either owned or worked on these boats. But Galena was dealt a bad hand. The Galena River always had been very narrow and silting only added to the problem. Galena tried dredging the river but their efforts were unsuccessful and by the 1860's the town had become just a backwater.

This scene has changed very little over the last ninety years and preserved along the levee are a number of warehouses dating from the era when Galena was a bustling river port. Historically the most significant of these structures is the Phineas Block Warehouse, the building just to the right of the horse and buggy. It was built sometime around 1827 making it one of the oldest surviving warehouses on the entire Mississippi River.

Post Office, Galena, Ill.

The Levee, Galena, Ill.

83
Blackjack Mine

The Blackjack Mine was the largest of the still sizable cluster of lead mines that dotted the landscape surrounding Galena back at the beginning of this century. Mining activity in this region reached its peak in the 1840's, and although buffeted by a series of reversals, the industry managed to survive and gradually took on a new form. Early on, most of Galena's mines were makeshift affairs that worked deposits just below ground. After 1870 the mines that were still operating were large and well capitalized, extracting lead from shafts sunk deep into the earth.

In the 1930's worldwide demand for lead plummeted and the number of mines here was reduced to a mere handful. World War II brought some increase in production, but subsequently demand continued to erode, and finally in the mid-1960's Galena lost its last remaining lead mine.

84
Mont Rest

This uniquely styled Bellevue, Iowa residence comes with a story that really is stranger then fiction. In the 1880's Seth Baker, a native of Bellevue, ventured to California in search of opportunity and fortune. His was a one in a million story because almost immediately he discovered an untapped vein of gold and became instantly wealthy. He returned to Bellevue and now as a man of means, built this house atop the city's highest hill in 1893. Unfortunately Baker was a compulsive gambler, and not a very good one. During an 1895 high stakes poker game at this home Baker, who was low on money, did the unthinkable and bet the deed to his house on what turned out to be a losing hand. Penniless, Baker left Bellevue and was never heard from again.

Over the next seventy years Mont Rest, as it came to be called, had a succession of owners before it was abandoned finally in the 1960's. Two decades later a young couple renovated this structure, converting it into what is now a very popular bed and breakfast. This very distinctive and storied landmark is located at 300 Spring Street.

The Blackjack Mine, Galena, Ill.

"MONT REST" BELLEVUE IA.

85
Steamer J.S.

Shown here striking an elegant pose at the Bellevue levee is the J.S., the most revered and celebrated excursion boat of its era. Bearing the initials of a man who owned and operated her, Captain John Streckfus, the J.S. first plied the Upper Mississippi in 1901. Every bit the equal of our modern Delta Queen, the J.S. was a 175-foot long floating palace filled with crystal chandeliers, velvet chairs and a myriad of other fine appointments. Passengers were entertained by an on-deck orchestra and at night this vessel was illuminated by 1,000 colored lights.

Everywhere she stopped the J.S. was greeted by throngs of people, but regrettably lady luck did not smile on this vessel. On June 18, 1910, while carrying 1,185 passengers, the J.S. caught fire on an excursion run between La Crosse, Wisconsin and Lansing, Iowa. Fortunately the captain was able to beach her on an island and all but two of its passengers scrambled to safety, but nothing could be done to save this fabled steamboat.

86 (121 l)
Twin Sisters

Resting on the edge of a bluff near Savanna, Illinois, this enormous stone pillar is one of the many natural wonders of what geologists refer to as the "Driftless Area". Extending on the river from about Winona, Minnesota to Clinton, Iowa, the Driftless Area was the one section of the midwest that was bypassed by the last glacier. As a consequence, this region is punctuated with a picturesque blending of towering bluffs, broad open valleys, and the occasional rock outcropping like the one pictured here.

The first white settlers to this section of the river named this 35-foot high rock the Twin Sisters because it consists of a pair of almost identical columns. This rock is now one of the prime attractions of Mississippi Palisades State Park, which is located four miles north of Savanna.

EXCURSION STEAMER "J.S." LEAVING BELLEVUE, Ia.

Twin Sisters SAVANNA Ill.

87
Savanna, Illinois

This bird's eye view showcases the area adjoining Savanna, Illinois' old levee. Positioned at the head of a major widening of the river 22 miles upstream from Clinton, Illinois, Savanna was initially settled in the mid-1830's. An inconsequential steamboat landing, Savanna was one of the first river communities to reach its zenith as a railroad town. Its once nearly stagnant economy came alive when the Illinois Central Railroad made it a division point in 1850. Towards the end of the Nineteenth Century, Savanna became a major terminal for a number of other regional rail carriers and in the years between 1900 and 1920 it had one of the busiest rail yards in the State of Illinois.
Savanna is still an important rail center but it now has a very diversified economy. Aside from the buildings immediately adjacent to the levee, which are no longer standing, this section of Savanna looks much like it did at the beginning of this century.

88
Fishermen at Savanna

These two gentlemen are a pair of commercial fishermen who, judging from the scene, have taken a brief break to pose for this photograph. Commercial fishing really didn't become well established on the upper Mississippi until the 1870's. By the end of the Nineteenth Century there were more than two thousand fishermen on these waters and over the last century the core elements of this industry have remained essentially the same. Then as now most fishermen work alone and use nets to haul in their catch. The vast majority have always resided in small communities and sold their fish to local distributors.
What has changed over the course of time is the type of fish caught. In 1900 the buffalo fish was the most important commercial fish on the Upper Mississippi and its tributaries. Over the next decade it was supplanted by the carp, which is still the predominant commercial fish on this waterway.

Bird's Eye View from North 4th Street,
Savanna, Ill.

River View, Savanna, Ill.

89 (122 u)
Raft at Clinton

This scene of a log raft entering the waters of Clinton is a singular testimony to a time when this town was the sawmill capitol of the world. The first sawmill was built here in the late 1850's and within the span of just over a decade Clinton had catapulted past other competing river towns to become the dominant player in the lumber market. A number of factors were responsible for this very rapid ascension. The lumber titans who built mills here, most notably W.J. Young, developed and improved the existing technology, creating gains in both productivity and cash flow. There was a steady inflow here of European immigrants willing to work in less then ideal conditions, and perhaps most important of all, Clinton was the closest point on the river to Chicago, which had an insatiable need for building lumber.

In 1892 an estimated 195 million board feet of lumber were produced in Clinton but the upriver pine forests were nearly depleted, and within two decades the town had but one remaining sawmill, which would soon go out of business. All that remains from that era are the elegant mansions built late in the Nineteenth Century by the town's lumber barons.

90
Eagle Point Park

This beguiling scene clearly demonstrates why Clinton's Eagle Point Park has a long-standing reputation as one of this river's premier overlooks. Dating back to the 1890's this park, which encompasses 200 acres, is situated at the extreme northern edge of Clinton. The park provided the first real opportunity for the townspeople of Clinton to connect with and enjoy the Mississippi, because as was the case with nearly every river town, there were railroad tracks running along the tracts of land immediately adjacent to the river.

Almost since its inception the park's star attraction, aside from its splendid views of the river, has been its floral displays. Over the course of the last several decades it has gained a number of new attractions, most notably a nature center. And, as its name suggests, this is an ideal spot to do some eagle watching.

CLINTON, IOWA. Lumbering on the Mississippi. 484

No 3. Eagle Point Park, overlooking Mississippi River, Clinton, Iowa. View 1.

91
Clinton Levee Scene

The joy and excitement of traveling by boat is clearly reflected in this view of an excursion party pouring out of a steamboat onto the Clinton levee. At the start of this century, river excursions were one of the most popular forms of recreation and entertainment in this river valley. Generally what happened in that era is that a group, like a club or fraternal organization, would rent a boat for a one or two day journey to some nearby town. To amuse themselves during the trip, excursionists held sing-a-longs, did plenty of dancing, and when there was nothing else to do they admired the scenery. Once they got to their destination they went on a tour of the town visiting its major landmarks, did some shopping, and if time permitted, stopped at a park for a picnic lunch.

Several factors contributed to the demise of these once so fashionable river excursions, but the primary reason was the automobile. After 1920, even if the roads were less than ideal, the Sunday drive was the thing that people looked forward to all week.

92
Old Stone House

This rather forsaken-looking structure is a landmark which predates by one year the founding of Clinton. A true pioneer dwelling, it was built in 1837 on a ridge overlooking the Mississippi River by William Thomas. Despite its size and the fact that it originally had only an earthen floor, the house also doubled as an inn, perhaps as late as the mid-1840's. We lack any real solid information to know if it was used as a station on the underground railroad as the caption indicates. The "Old Stone House" reemerged from a long period of obscurity when it was remodeled and converted into a tourist cabin in the 1920's.

Over the last half century this structure has been modified and altered to the point where it has lost nearly all of its historic integrity. Now a private residence, this ancient Clinton landmark is located at 850 S. Bluff Boulevard.

MISSISSIPPI RIVER EXCURSION ARRIVING AT CLINTON, IOWA

The Old Stone House, Clinton, Iowa.
This house was a place of refuge for fugitive slaves during slavery days.

93 (122 l)
Bow Boat

The vessel in the foreground straddling a log raft passing a marina at Lyons, Iowa, was the river's most specialized steamboat. Called bow boats, they served as kind of a guiding mechanism for the steamer that was pushing a raft. For a large raft they were virtually indispensable because the river back then was cluttered with obstacles ranging from snags to hundreds upon hundreds of small islands.

Needless to say, piloting a bow boat was one of the most dangerous jobs on the river. Any kind of misstep and you could wind up impaled on a bridge pier or colliding with another vessel. Sometimes luck was your only friend. In an 1890 incident that rivermen talked about for decades, a bow boat was pushed onto the draw pier of a Clinton bridge and then was lifted all the way up to the bridgedeck. Miraculously, although the boat sustained heavy damage, its crew were able to walk away from the accident with just a few minor cuts and bruises.

94
Fulton, Illinois

One would have to assume that this photographic view showing the commercial district of Fulton, Illinois was taken on a Sunday morning. This community which sits on the river directly opposite from Clinton, Iowa was first settled in 1837 and named in honor of Robert Fulton, who designed the first steamboat. Fulton's growth was quite anemic until the 1850's when it developed into a lumbering center. Like its counterpart across the river, Fulton had sawmills that operated 24-hours a day. In the 1870's Fulton also became a major exporter of earthen stoneware and at one juncture it had four pottery plants.

For all practical purposes modern day Fulton has become a suburb of Clinton. Unfortunately as a consequence much of the life has been drained from its old commercial district and many of these buildings along this street have a tired and weathered look.

Log Raft, Steamer and Bow Boat, Mississippi River, Lyons, Iowa.

Fourth St., Looking North, Fulton, Ill.

95
Fulton, Illinois - Ferry

This scene, which shows a group of passengers disembarking from a ferry at Fulton, Illinois, rekindles memories of a time when ferries played an essential role in the day-to-day life of almost every Upper Mississippi community. In the pre-railroad epoch, ferries provided the only regular lifeline to the outside world for most river communities. The fate of a town often hinged on the quality and reliability of its ferry service. Ferriage at Fulton began with the initial settlement of this area in the 1830's, and over the next four decades it wasn't all that unusual to have three ferry operators competing for business between here and Lyons, Iowa. After the railroad had taken away all of their profits, they were dealt an all but fatal death blow when the wagon bridge, shown here, was completed in 1891. This particular ferry was owned by William Harlock, a determined entrepreneur who established himself here in 1900. Harlock operated what would be Fulton's last ferry all the way up to 1918 when he left with his boat to haul freight on the Hennepin Canal.

96
Ice Harvesting

This wintry scene shows a work crew harvesting ice on the river near the levee at Lyons, Iowa. One tends to forget how reliant we once were on ice cut from bodies of water like the Mississippi River to preserve our food. Ice blocks were cut by using five-foot long heavily reinforced hand saws. Once cut, the ice was hauled away in wagons to a shed where it was packed in sawdust. In some communities like Lyons the local ice house was built right on the edge of the river. The slide in the right corner of this picture was actually a conveyor belt that moved the ice directly from the river into the ice house. Such an arrangement eliminated a lot of back-breaking labor and made it possible to store more ice.

Modern refrigeration brought a quick end to ice harvesting. On the Upper Mississippi the 1930's was the last decade in which ice was extracted from the river.

2564 Ferry Landing, Fulton, Ill.

JOHN B. HANSON

The mule bridge between Fulton and Lyons.

Preparing for
Ice Supply on
Mississippi,
Lyons, Iowa.

97
Albany, Illinois

One has to wonder why the photographer selected this tree-obscured setting to shows us Albany, Illinois. Located just downstream from Clinton, Iowa, Albany was founded in 1840 by a group of land speculators. The town got off to a very positive beginning. In just over a decade it had grown into a mature riverport of well over 1,000 residents and many thought it would eventually become a major trade center. But one fateful day reshaped the course of its history. On the evening of June 3, 1860 a monstrous tornado plowed a path of destruction right through the heart of Albany leveling most of its homes and businesses. Some rebuilding occurred but Albany lost whatever hopes it had of becoming a great metropolis.

Over the last three decades, Albany has experienced a sustained period of growth and revival. Tourism has played only a minor role and the primary catalyst has been its ability to feed off the growth of neighboring Clinton.

98
Port Byron View From River

Taken one would assume from a steamer parked in the middle of the Mississippi, this view showcases what was the main business district of Port Byron, Illinois. Positioned at a point on the river just upstream from Le Claire, Iowa, Port Byron was platted as a town in 1836 by a group of settlers who named it in honor of the British poet Lord Byron. Settled initially by transplants from New England, this community first took on the appearance of a real town with the opening of a hotel here in 1840. Port Byron is perhaps best known for its lime, which was the town's leading industry from the 1840's to well into the Twentieth Century.

What is interesting about this vignette is that if you take a close look you'll notice that all of the buildings have doorways facing the river. One has to remember that back in the steamboat era nearly all goods coming into a town arrived by boat, and merchants placed their doorways accordingly. None of the buildings shown here have survived and this section of the town's riverfront is now a marina and park.

Main Street, Albany, Ill.
Mississippi River in the
distance

FALLS ST. ANTHONY, MINNEAPOLIS, MINN.

FLOUR MILLING DISTRICT, MINNEAPOLIS, MINN.

The Stone arch bridge and West side milling District, Minneapolis, Minn.

MINNEHAHA FALLS, MINNEAPOLIS, MINN.

Dakota County Court House, Hastings, Minn.

Vermillion Falls, Hastings, Minn.

Red Wing from Wisconsin Shore

BARN'S BLUFF, SHOWING STAIRWAY, RED WING, MINN.

"ON THE CHICAGO, MILWAUKEE & ST. PAUL RAILWAY"

LAKE PEPIN, MINN., UPPER MISSISSIPPI RIVER.

68988

114

2905. Levee Park, Winona, Minn.

Winter Sports, Winona, Minn.—28

Steamer Quincy sunk near Trempeleau, Wis., on the Mississippi River

8326. Public Bath House and Swimming Pool, La Crosse, Wi

Grand Dad Bluff,
La Crosse, Wis.

Lansing and Mississippi from the Bluffs, Lansing, Iowa.

Birdseye View of Harpers Ferry Iowa.

THE LEWIS HOTEL, MC GREGOR, IOWA.

THE OLD DESERTED SHOT TOWER, DUBUQUE, IOWA

Dubuque, Ia. U. S. A.
Fourth Street Hill Elevator.
300 feet above city.

MAJESTIC THEATRE, DUBUQUE.

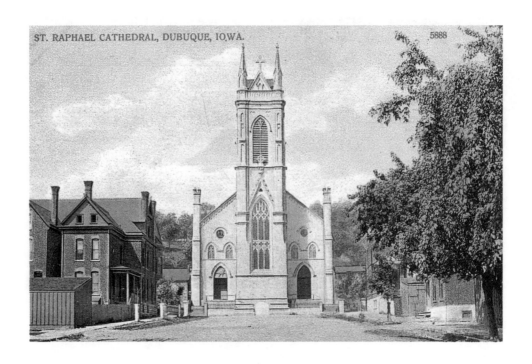

ST. RAPHAEL CATHEDRAL, DUBUQUE, IOWA. 5888

The Levee, Galena, Ill.

E. W. KEMPTER, PUB. NO 10

Twin Sisters SAVANNA Ill.

U. S. 500.

CLINTON, IOWA.   Lumbering on the Mississippi.   48

Log Raft, Steamer and Bow Boat, Mississippi River, Lyons, Iowa.

The Green Tree, Le Claire, Iowa.

Battle Monument, Campbell's Island, near Moline, Ill.

BETTENDORF STEEL CAR WORKS, BETTENDORF, IOWA.

ROCK ISLAND–DAVENPORT FERRY

MARKET SQUARE, ROCK ISLAND, ILL.

BLACKHAWK INN, ROCK ISLAND, ILL.

AR VIEW—OLD COL. GEO. DAVENPORT HOME ROCK ISLAND ARSENAL BEFORE RESTORATION
ROCK ISLAND, ILL.

Rock Island Arsenal Shops, Rock Island, Ill.

Camping on the Mississippi River, near Muscatine, Iowa.

Snake Alley, Burlington, Iowa.

Crapo Park, Burlington, Iowa.

FORT MADISON, IOWA.   Lee Co. Court House, Jail & Sheriff's Residence

Bird's-Eye View of Nauvoo, Ill.

Residence of C. R. Joy, Keokuk, Ia.

Keokuk and Hamilton Bridge, Keokuk, Ia.

MAIN ST. N. LA GRANGE, MO.

Boat Landing, Quincy, Ill.

Fountain and Band Stand
Washington Park, Quincy, Ill

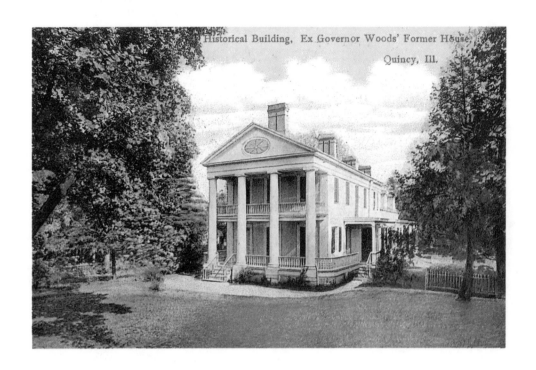

Historical Building, Ex Governor Woods' Former House, Quincy, Ill.

Villa Kathrine, Quincy, Ill.

Mark Twain Monument,
Riverview Park, Hannibal, Mo.

Mark Twain's Home, Hannibal, Mo.

Home of Huckleberry Finn, Hannibal, Mo.

P.26608

CRUIKSHANK RESIDENCE, HANNIBAL, MO.

LOVERS LEAP AND MISSISSIPPI RIVER, HANNIBAL, MO.

Lovejoy Monument, Alton, Ill.

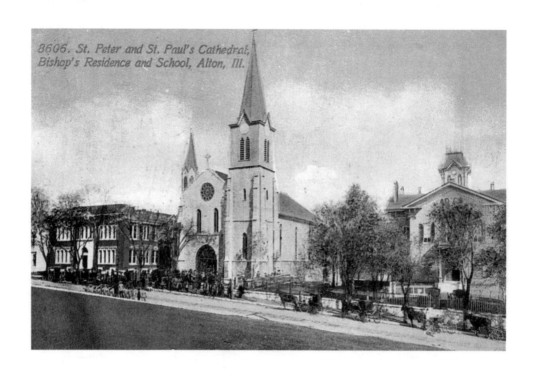

8606. St. Peter and St. Paul's Cathedral, Bishop's Residence and School, Alton, Ill.

12331. Intake Tower, Water Works, Chain of Rocks, St. Louis, Mo.

EADS BRIDGE, ST. LOUIS, MO.

7985. City Hall, St. Louis, Mo.

UNION STATION, ST. LOUIS, MO.

TOTAL DIMENSIONS, 820.606 FEET
COVERING 11 ACRES

Bronze Statue of St. Louis Art Hill-Forest Park. St. Louis. U. S. A.

Vandeventer Place, St. Louis, Mo.

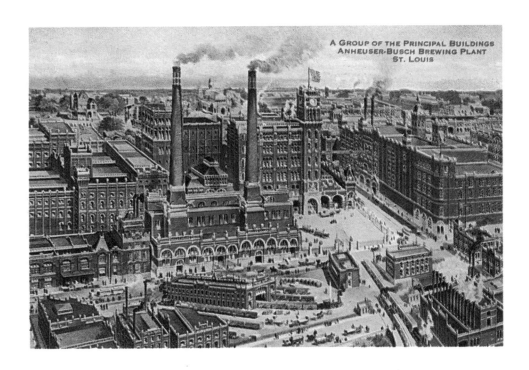

A GROUP OF THE PRINCIPAL BUILDINGS
ANHEUSER-BUSCH BREWING PLANT
ST. LOUIS

Tower Rock near Murphysboro, Ill.

Grand Tower, Ill.

View on Themis Street, Cape Girardeau, Mo.

Missouri State Normal, Cape Girardeau, Mo.

"THE HEWER" DRINKING FOUNTAIN, CAIRO, ILL.

99
Port Byron – Lime Kiln

This splendid view shows us one of the many lime kilns that once dotted the landscape of Port Byron, Illinois. Converting limestone into lime was once the predominant economic activity for small towns in the Upper Mississippi Valley. Refus Chase, a stonemason, is credited with building the town's first kiln sometime around 1840. Most of the limestone that was produced in Port Byron was packed in barrels and then transported in steamers to communities as far away as St. Paul and St. Louis.

The kiln shown here was owned by Henry C. Trent, who was also the town grocer. Trent built this facility in the early 1880's and he operated it until 1907 when he was bought out by one of his competitors. Over time, those who succeeded Trent weren't able to compete in the marketplace after the introduction of hydrated lime and by the mid-1930's Port Byron had lost all its lime kilns.

100
Port Byron Congregational Church

The Port Byron Congregational Church is the quintessential Nineteenth Century small town church. This fellowship, which had twelve original members, was organized in 1849 by Reverend Julius Reed, a home missionary from Iowa. Their first services were held in an old school and then somehow they put together a funding package to build this church, which cost $2,700, and was completed in 1856. The church was the model of simplicity and its only extravagant appointment was a 500-pound church bell cast in Boston, Massachusetts.

For most of this century the basic issue for this church has been one of survival and rarely has it had more then 100 members. The most drastic alteration to this brick edifice occurred in the 1930's when the entire front was rebuilt to accommodate a new highway. This picturesque little church is located at 202 South High Street.

101
LeClaire, Iowa

This view of Main Street in LeClaire, Iowa was taken in 1906. Located 17 miles upstream from Davenport, Iowa at the head of the Rock Island Rapids, LeClaire was founded in 1837 and named in honor of Antoine LeClaire. Almost from its inception, LeClaire played a key role in the economic development of this river. For most of the steamboat era it served as the base of operations for a highly specialized group of rivermen called the "rapids pilots." Using their local knowledge of currents and rock formations, these men guided boats through the dangerous Rock Island Rapids. Beginning in 1856 LeClaire was also home to one of the river's largest boatyards. The town's most famous native son was a non-riverman, "Buffalo Bill," Cody who lived here from 1848 to 1854.

Several decades ago Main Street, which runs parallel to the river, was renamed Cody Road. Although most of the buildings in this scene were razed in the 1970's, Cody Road contains a number of historically significant homes built in the mid-Nineteenth Century by LeClaire's rivermen.

102 (123 u)
LeClaire - Green Tree

For the better part of a century, this quite ordinary elm tree was the most cherished and important landmark in LeClaire, Iowa. Stationed at the foot of the LeClaire levee, the tree became a gathering place in the 1850's for the town's "Rafting Pilots" who steered boats through the treacherous currents of the Upper Rapids. They would congregate underneath the tree swapping stories and the latest river gossip while waiting for the next downriver boat to pick them up. There is a lot of folklore regarding what came to be called the Green Tree, but one true story is that LeClaire managed to convince a railroad to reroute their proposed line through this community to avoid damaging their sacrosanct landmark.

Alas, like millions of other elms, the Green Tree contracted Dutch Elm Disease and it was chopped down in 1962. Much of its story is presented in the Buffalo Bill Museum which is situated on the site of the depot, pictured here near the foot of River Drive.

Main Street, Le Claire, Iowa.

The Green Tree, Le Claire, Iowa.

103 (123 l)
Campbell's Island Monument

This island monument commemorates the one and only battle fought on the Upper Mississippi during the War of 1812. The encounter occurred on July 20, 1814 when a flotilla of keelboats commanded by Major John Campbell headed upriver from St. Louis to reinforce the garrison at Prairie du Chien. While passing what is now the Quad Cities, they ran into a storm and Campbell decided to beach his boats on a small island. Lying in ambush were a group of Soc warriors led by Chief Blackhawk, and in a brief but bloody skirmish, 14 Americans were killed and 17 were wounded, including Campbell. Shaken and demoralized, the contingent had no other option but to return to St. Louis. The monument, which is a small shaft of granite, was erected on the southern end of Campbell's Island in 1905. This island, which is now a state park, sits on the river adjacent to East Moline, Illinois.

104 (124 u)
Bettendorf Car Works

This mammoth industrial plant gave rise to the last and most obscure member of the cluster of towns that comprise the Quad Cities - Bettendorf, Iowa. Prior to the building of this plant, Davenport, Iowa's adjoining eastern neighbor was Gilbert, a tiny farming hamlet. In 1902 two intrepid entrepreneurs, William and Joseph Bettendorf, decided to build a plant where they would manufacture wagon parts in Gilbert. One year later Gilbert was renamed Bettendorf, and simultaneously the two brothers decided to switch gears and build railroad cars at their new facility. They were tremendously successful and soon other companies were attracted to this community and over the next two decades Bettendorf was one of the fastest growing towns on the Mississippi.
The Bettendorf Car Works, the colossus which created a town, went out of business in 1932, one of the many casualties of the Great Depression. This facility, which was located at the foot of 18th street, was utilized for a lengthy period of time by the J.I. Case Company before it was finally razed in the 1980's.

Battle Monument, Campbell's Island
near Moline, Ill.

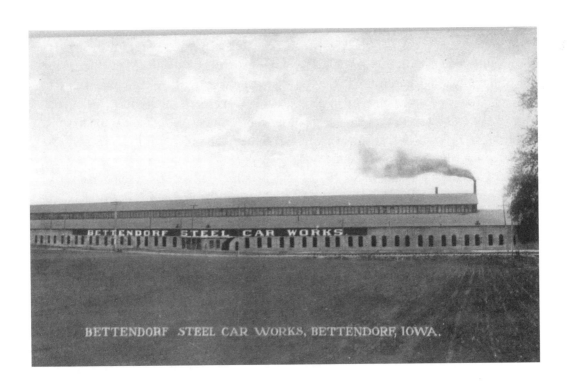

BETTENDORF STEEL CAR WORKS, BETTENDORF, IOWA.

105
Sacred Heart Cathedral

Sacred Heart Cathedral is part of an unbroken tradition that dates back to one of the founding fathers of Davenport, Antoine LeClaire. A former Indian interpreter, LeClaire was one of the original settlers of Davenport in 1836 and its leading citizen for a number of decades. Devoutly religious, he donated a large parcel of land upon which was built St. Marguerite's Church in 1856. Under his sponsorship, the parish prospered and in 1881, when Davenport became an Episcopal see, the new bishop deemed it the most appropriate site for a new Cathedral. The old church was dismantled and in 1891 work was completed on this large new edifice.

Traditional in its design, this building's most interesting feature is its limestone brick facade. Sacred Heart Cathedral is located on East Tenth Street between Iowa and LeClaire.

106
Central Park - Davenport

Here is a bucolic and engaging scene of youngsters striking a pose on a summer day at Davenport's Central Park. Initially, city parks were viewed as a way for urban dwellers to commune with nature in an unspoiled pasture-like setting. Established in 1885 on the site of the city's old fairgrounds, Central Park was very much in keeping with that tradition. The park was comprised of 33 acres of lush greenery and its only concessions to the outside world were a pavilion and conservatory. But even paradise could have its problems, because in 1907 this rustic well had to be filled in after an analysis revealed its contaminated water was spreading typhoid fever.

Renamed Vander Veer Park in the 1920's, this park has evolved in the same manner as most urban parks, and thus today it has all the prerequisite updated features including a swimming pool and a large playground area. The crown jewel of Davenport's park system, it is located near the intersection of Locust and Brady.

13206. Central Park, Davenport, Ia.

149

107 (124 l)
T.J. Robinson Ferry

The T.J. Robinson was one of a long list of ferryboats that ran between Rock Island and Davenport dating back to a time when these towns didn't even exist. Only a few families were living in this area in 1825 when George Davenport began operating a ferry service. at what is now Arsenal Island. By the time Rock Island and Davenport became established towns there were several ferry companies locked in an intense battle for business. Finally, in the late 1850's a winner emerged in that competition, the Rock Island-Davenport Ferry Company, which for many decades had a monopoly. One of the founding partners of this company was T.J. Robinson, who died in 1899. To honor his memory the remaining owners christened this boat (formerly the "Augusta"), which they purchased and began operating in 1902. The Robinson was one of the largest ferryboats of its era and one of the most photographed steamers on the river.

This famed steamer was eventually sold to a ferry operator at Helena Arkansas in 1915. Its departure by no means marked the end of ferry service here, which continued into the 1950's.

108 (125 u)
Market Square

This view of Rock Island's outdoor marketplace is a vivid illustration of how different urban streets were in the pre-car era. When streets were the domain of the horse and buggy it wasn't all that uncommon to have structures like this pavilion in the middle of a thoroughfare because they really didn't impede the flow of traffic. Standing on the 1600 block of Second Avenue, this pavilion, which dates from about 1880, served the community in a variety of ways. Vendors sold fruit and produce from the arched space at its base, and the upper section was utilized both as a bandstand and speaking platform. If you are wondering about that large pit adjacent to the pavilion, it was probably a watering hole for horses.

When the automobile replaced the horse and buggy, all the old street structures were quickly torn down. Rock Island lost its pavilion sometime around 1910 and Market Square lost some of its history.

ROCK ISLAND–DAVENPORT FERRY

MARKET SQUARE, ROCK ISLAND, ILL.

109
Augustana College

Augustana College is a reflection of the Swedish heritage that has long been one of the defining characteristics of Rock Island, Illinois. This school was chartered in 1860 by the Evangelical Lutheran Synod of Northern, Illinois to train young men for a career in Lutheran ministry. Augustana's first years were anything but easy because it wasn't able to find what it needed most, a town with a large Swedish population. By 1870 several communities were seeking the school but Rock Island carried the day on the strength of its Swedish roots, and because it offered Augustana a choice tract of land for its new campus. The institution received its first class of students here in 1876 and by the time this picture was taken it had matured into one of the country's most prestigious seminaries.

Of the buildings pictured here the one on the right is still standing and it now houses the school's administrative offices. Augustana College is situated on Zion Hill at the corner of 38th and 7th Avenue.

110 (125 l)
Watch Tower Inn

This inn was one of the main attractions at Watch Tower Park, Rock Island's renowned "end of the line" amusement park. The antecedent of our modern theme park, the end of the line amusement park was an essential component of nearly every big city streetcar company which used them as a way to boost ridership on the weekends. And as the name suggests, they were usually situated at the end point of a company's transit line. Watch Tower Park was developed in 1882 by the Rock Island Railway Company and was situated on a 200-acre tract of land on a bluff overlooking the Rock River. The park had all the usual staples of any good amusement center including a Tunnel of Love, assorted games of skill, several merry-go-rounds, and of course, a roller coaster. In its heyday, at the turn-of-the-century, the park drew upwards of 15,000 people a day.

Watch Tower Park, like other amusement parks, was unable to resist the onslaught of the automobile, and after years of declining attendance it closed in 1925. Two years later the State of Illinois purchased the park, and after razing all its old structures transformed it into what is today Blackhawk State Park. Once the site of an Indian village, this park is located in the southwestern corner of Rock Island.

BLACKHAWK INN, ROCK ISLAND, ILL.

111
Watch Tower Park - Toboggan Slide

We are looking at a close-up view of the "Shoot the Chutes", Watch Tower Park's signature amusement ride. This thrill-a-minute ride was invented in 1884 by J.P. Newbery, a resident of Rock Island. The ride was a 100-foot long toboggan slide which ran from the top of a steep bluff down to where it met the Rock River. Riders boarded a flat bottom boat, which plunged down a greased track at speeds of up to 80 miles an hour. The real thrill of course came when the boat slammed into the river, giving everyone inside a tremendous jolt as they were sprayed with water.
The "Shoot the Chutes" is still one of the prime attractions at nearly every modern theme park. They're a far cry, of course, from the original Watch Tower Park ride which deposited its riders into a real river.

112
Rock Island Bridge Monument

Covered over with moss, this tangled slab of rock is the last surviving remnant of the first railroad bridge to span the Mississippi River. Its story is really about who would control the Mississippi—the fledgling railroad industry or the rivermen with their steamboats. The brewing storm began in 1853 when the Rock Island Railroad announced it was going to build a bridge over the river between Rock Island and Davenport. Citing the hazards it would pose to navigation, the steamship lines launched an unsuccessful drive to block its construction. Their fears were borne out because on May 6, 1856, just 15 days after the bridge was completed, the Effie Afton, a small steamer, hit one of the bridge's piers and exploded into a ball of flames. Now with the ammunition they needed, the steamship lines initiated a lawsuit that would block the railroad companies from building any additional bridges over the Mississippi. The case went all the way to the U.S. Supreme Court, who ruled in favor of the railroad companies, and by 1880, just as the steamboat owners had feared, the railroads had seized control of the freight business along the Mississippi River.
The original Rock Island Bridge was torn down and replaced by a new structure in 1872. This surviving section of the bridge was recast several years ago into a memorial which is located on the north end of Arsenal Island.

LOOKING UP TOBOGGAN SLIDE
BLACKHAWKS WATCH TOWER

Old Stone Abutment of Old Bridge, Rock Island Arsenal

113 (126 u)
Davenport House

This beleaguered looking structure was the home of a trailblazing pioneer settler, Colonel George Davenport. In 1816 Davenport became the first white settler of what would eventually become the Quad Cities, when he arrived here as the supply agent for Fort Armstrong. Gaining the trust of the local Indians, he entered the fur business and then over the course of the next several decades, he was responsible for the founding of several towns, including both Davenport and Rock Island. He became an accomplished riverboat pilot, and was the region's first postmaster. With a vast fortune at his disposal, Davenport built this large frame house in 1833. Twelve years later on July 4, 1845, it became the site of his untimely death when he was brutally murdered by a gang of thieves.

In the years that followed, Davenport's widow lived in the house for a brief time before selling it to the Army, which used it as a warehouse and then it slowly fell into disrepair. In 1906 the house was rebuilt by the Old Settlers Association and in the 1970's a second restoration was initiated by a group of local citizens. This distinguished landmark is located at the north end of Arsenal Island.

114 (126 l)
Rock Island Arsenal

These nondescript government buildings represent the final phase in the U.S. Army's long-standing occupation of Arsenal Island. In 1816 a battalion of troop under the command of Col. William Lawrence arrived at this large island and built Fort Armstrong. The island was strategically situated at the foot of the Upper Rapids, midway on the river between St. Louis and Fort Snelling. Over the fort's 20-year existence, until it was finally abandoned in 1836, it served as a jumping off point for settlers heading upriver and it planted the seed from which sprang both Davenport and Rock Island. The Army reestablished a presence on the island in 1862, operating a quite infamous Civil War prison where nearly 2,000 men died of disease or starvation. Following the war, the island was chosen as the site for an arsenal and construction was initiated on these ten buildings where small arms and ammunition were manufactured for years and up to the time of the Korean War.

Arsenal Island is still an active military base and, if you're wondering, these buildings still stand. On the island, easily accessed by car, are a number of historic sites including two military cemeteries and a monument which marks the site of Fort Armstrong.

EAR VIEW – OLD COL. GEO. DAVENPORT HOME ROCK ISLAND ARSENAL BEFORE RESTORATION
ROCK ISLAND, ILL.

Rock Island Arsenal Shops, Rock Island, Ill.

115
McKee and Bliven Button Factory

The McKee and Bliven Button Factory is one of the last surviving structures from an era when Muscatine could rightly lay claim to be the "Pearl Button Capital of the World". Muscatine became the dominant player in this industry thanks to a local resident named J.F. Boepple, who in 1891 developed a lathe which made it possible to mass produce buttons from clam shells. Thanks to his initiative, by 1900 this city had 39 button factories employing almost 3,500 people. Gradually this number began to shrink but even today, ten percent of the buttons produced in this country come from Muscatine. The McKee and Bliven Company was founded in 1895, the same year in which this plant was built. Almost from its inception, this company was the town's leading button manufacturer and back at the beginning of this century, several hundred people were employed here. Now churning out plastic buttons, this historic factory is located at 1000 Hershey Avenue.

116
First Presbyterian Church

The First Presbyterian Church is one of a handful of well-preserved pre-Civil War buildings in Muscatine. A group of eleven residents organized the church in the winter of 1842 and the first worship services were conducted in a river meeting hall. In 1849 the congregation built their first church, but it wasn't long before they outgrew it and in 1856, after a successful fund raising drive, work was begun on the present house of worship. Due to unforeseen delays in the construction process it took nearly three years to build the church which was finally dedicated in the Spring of 1859. The church's most notable design features are its pointed arched windows and its corner buttresses. Time has done little to alter the original character of this historic church and the only significant change occurred in 1912 when a Sunday school building was erected on an adjoining lot. One of the first buildings in Muscatine to be placed on the National Register of Historic Places, the First Presbyterian Church is located at the corner of Fourth and Iowa.

McKee & Bliven Button Factory, Muscatine, Iowa

First Presbyterian Church Muscatine Iowa.

117
Muscatine Baseball Game

This card documents one of the great moments in the history of Muscatine, its first professional baseball game. The date was May 17, 1910 and the Muscatine Camels, as they were called, were matched up against the Freeport Pretzels, both of whom were members of the newly formed Northern Association. Back in that day baseball reigned supreme as America's number one spectator sport, so having a pro team was really something to crow about. Prior to the game the town staged a huge parade in the team's honor that included a brass band and a host of local dignitaries.

The game itself, with 2,581 fans packed into this small park, was a wild and noisy affair. Many people had megaphones and practically everyone else had some type of noise-maker. The hometowners came away happy because the Camels were the victors in a 4 to 0 game.

118 (127 u)
Camping

One feels an instinctive yearning to go back in time and join these people who are camped out along the river somewhere near Muscatine, Iowa. Camping is one of the Upper Mississippi's most time-honored traditions, but there have been a number of subtle changes over the course of time. One of the more distinctive differences was that back at the turn-of-the-century everyone in the family got dressed up even when they were camping, with the women wearing cotton dresses and the men always attired in long sleeve shirts. What was also different was that much of the camping was done on islands because is this pre-dam era the river had so many more islands than it does today.

Times back then were indeed much simpler and camping activities were centered on such things as collecting berries and picking wildflowers. One might also add that, like their modern counterparts, campers of that era were locked in a never-ending battle with one of man's most annoying foes, the mosquito.

BALL GROUNDS, MUSCATINE IOWA

Camping on the Mississippi River, near Muscatine, Iowa

119
Abe Lincoln Hotel - New Boston Illinois

This card showcases the Abe Lincoln Hotel the oldest surviving commercial building in New Boston, Illinois. Situated on the opposite shore from the mouth of the Iowa River, New Boston was established as a town in 1834. The original survey of the town was conducted by a future American President, Abraham Lincoln. Unfortunately New Boston, despite its early aspirations never matured into a steamboat landing. The brightest decade for this town occurred in the 1890's when it had one of the area's largest button factories.

Originally called the Fleming House, the Abe Lincoln Hotel was built in the mid 1860's. For many years the social hub of this sleepy river village, it was utilized as a hotel all the way up to the 1970's. This classic Nineteenth Century hotel, which is now an antique store, is located at the west end of Main Street.

120
Keithsburg, Illinois

This card provides a close-up view of the main business district in Keithsburg, Illinois. Situated on the river about midway between Muscatine and Burlington, Iowa, Keithsburg was founded in 1837 by Robert Keith, a Scottish immigrant. Settlement progressed slowly and it didn't become a full-fledged town until 1850, and then over the next decade Keithsburg developed into a moderately successful riverport. The town's most prosperous period were the years between 1880 and 1910, when it had a number of local manufacturing plants, including a wagonmaker, flour mill, and several cigar factories. For most of this century Keithsburg, like many of its west central Illinois neighbors, has seen its economy stagnate because of its relatively isolated geographic position.

This commercial strip has survived nearly intact and these Nineteenth Century buildings are in remarkably good condition. In 1986 this block and nearly all of Keithsburg's old commercial district were added to the National Register of Historic Places.

3rd and Main Sts., Keithsburg, Ill.

121
Oquawka, Illinois

These three buildings are located on the east end of Schuyler Street in Oquawka, Illinois. Sporting an Indian name meaning "Yellow Banks", Oquawka was platted as a town in 1836. Located 13 miles upstream from Burlington, Iowa this community grew rapidly into a bustling commercial center and by 1850 it had nearly 2,000 residents. One measure of Oquawka's early stature is that Stephen A. Douglas and Abraham Lincoln held one of their senatorial debates here in 1858. But this once shimmering star quickly faded after this area was crisscrossed by railroads in the 1860's and at the end of the Nineteenth Century Oquawka's population had dipped to just over 1,000.

Oquawka has managed to preserve much of its heritage and this block still plays a vital part in the life of this community. The building on the left still houses a barber shop. Adjoining it is the community's old opera house, which now houses a newspaper office and craft shop and the building on the far right, once a bakery, has become a pharmacy.

122
First Congregational Church

The First Congregational Church is one of Burlington's oldest and most distinguished landmarks. This church was founded in 1838, by a group of transplanted New Englanders, just five years after Burlington became a town. For it first eight years the congregation worshipped at a local school and then in 1846 they were blessed by the arrival of Reverend William Salter. A brilliant preacher, who in his later years became a noted historian, Reverend Salter is closely identified with this church because he served as its pastor until 1910 when he died at the age of 89. In the first year of Salter's ministry the congregation moved into a frame church and two decades later work was begun on this church which was completed in 1870.

The church, which has a limestone frame exterior, possesses a number of notable features including a gabled entry, a fine array of stained glass windows and a distinctive medieval style tower. Most of its interior was rebuilt after a disastrous 1899 fire. This handsome and historic church is located at 331 N. Fourth Street.

Street Scene, Oquawka, Ill. "5.   Bretton.

CONGREGATIONAL CHURCH, BURLINGTON, IOWA.

2182-7

123 (127 l)
Snake Alley

No, your eyes aren't deceiving you—this downhill spiral is an actual street, Burlington's fabled Snake Alley. Contrary to what one might think, the city fathers had a practical purpose in mind when they laid out Snake Alley in 1894. What they were aiming to achieve was a way for horses to get better traction as they maneuvered down this steep hill. Although the concept may have been a little unorthodox, they certainly created something unique because in the span of one block, Snake Alley makes five half curves and two quarter curves.

Once the automobile replaced the horse and buggy, Snake Alley was transformed from a street into an odd anachronism. It gradually became a tourist attraction thanks in large measure to "Believe It or Not" columnist Robert C. Ripley, who named it the "Crookedest Street in the World." Now Burlington's preeminent landmark and the site of numerous local festivals and events, Snake Alley is situated at the corner of Sixth and Washington.

124
Boeck Packing Plant

The Boeck and Company Packing Plant pictured here was one of the last survivors from a time back in the Nineteenth Century when every Upper Mississippi town of any consequence has at least two or three family-owned slaughterhouses. Until mobile refrigeration units were finally perfected in the 1890's, meat packing and distribution had to be a localized business or otherwise everyone would have been eating tainted meat. Like so many of his contemporaries in this industry, George Boeck, the man who founded this company, was a first generation European immigrant. Boeck began selling meat at Burlington in 1864 when he was only 23, and by the 1880's he had become one of the town's most successful and admired businessmen.

Around 1900 the meat packing industry experienced a rapid consolidation with a few large companies based in major urban centers like Chicago dominating the market. The Boeck Company folded shortly after this picture was taken and in 1914 the plant was purchased by the Burlington Vinegar and Pickle Works.

Snake Alley, Burlington, Iowa.

5156. Boeck & Co. Packing Plant, Burlington, Iowa.

BOECK & COMPANY

125 (128 u)
Crapo Park

One look at this enchanting scene and you can understand immediately why Crapo Park has long been Burlington's most valued and treasured asset. The park, which sits on a high bluff overlooking the Mississippi River at the southern tip of the city, was established in 1895 thanks to a fund raising effort led by Philip Crapo. Burlington got the chance to showcase this park almost immediately because the following year it was the site of Iowa's Semi-Centennial celebration. Many of the events for this extravaganza were held in the building shown here that was called the Coliseum, which was demolished in 1920.

Over the course of the last century the park acquired many new features, including an outdoor pool and several shelters, but what really makes it special is that it has retained all the delightful qualities of a Nineteenth Century park.

126
Iowa State Penitentiary at Fort Madison

This view takes us inside the ominous confines of a rather ignoble river attraction, the Iowa State Penitentiary, located on the outskirts of Fort Madison, Iowa. One of the first steps taken after Iowa gained its statehood was choosing Fort Madison as the site for its first prison. The decision was facilitated by Fort Madison's willingness to donate a ten acre parcel of land for the proposed facility. Established in 1839, the prison was little more than a farming compound in its earliest phase, and then progressively more and more buildings were added and eventually encircled by this medieval looking wall. Now a maximum security prison, this penitentiary hasn't changed all that much in the last ninety odd years. One of the state's oldest landmarks, it is situated in the northeast corner of Fort Madison.

Crapo Park, Burlington, Iowa.

BIRD'S-EYE-VIEW OF PRISON SHOPS,
FORT MADISON, IOWA

127
Atlee Sawmill

This is a significant historic picture because the Atlee's Lumber Mill was for the first several decades of this century one of the last surviving sawmills on the Upper Mississippi. In the period between 1860 and 1890 there were hundreds of sawmills operating along the river between St. Paul and St. Louis. A town the size of Fort Madison might have a dozen or more mills and those who owned them were usually the wealthiest men in their communities. The Atlee Mill, which was founded in 1832 by John C. Atlee, had like many of the larger mills its own fleet of steamboats and during its peak years in the 1880's it was cranking out nearly 60,000 feet of lumber per day.

The Atlee Mill closed out the era of logging on the Upper Mississippi when one of its boats pushed the last log raft down stream from Hudson, Wisconsin to Fort Madison in 1915. For a brief period the company, which was located at the southwestern corner of the city, continued to produce wood products and then it was transformed into a lumber yard that was finally liquidated by its owner in the mid-1950's.

128
Santa Fe Railroad Bridge

The Santa Fe Railroad Bridge, which crossed the river at Fort Madison, was unique even in its own day because it also doubled as a single deck toll bridge. The Santa Fe Railroad in an effort to promote good will added two one-way lanes to accommodate the general public when they built this bridge, which was completed in 1888. Their toll fees were pretty much in line with the rates being charged by ferry operators in the area. The fees were as follows: twenty cents for a two-horse buggy, twenty-five cents for a two-horse vehicle, and pedestrians were charged a nickel.

In 1924, just thirty-six years after it was built, the old Santa Fe Bridge was declared unsafe and three years later it was replaced by an elaborately designed and very expensive steel bridge. The present structure is also a toll bridge, but unlike its predecessor it has separate decks for cars and trains.

ATLEES' LUMBER MILLS, FORT MADISON, IOWA

Santa Fe R. R. Bridge, Fort Madison, Iowa.

129 (128 l)
Lee County Courthouse

The Lee County Courthouse is Fort Madison's most enduring landmark. In 1836 Fort Madison was selected as the county seat. Disgruntled about not winning this prize, several adjoining communities managed to get the state to reconsider its decision and the issue was left unresolved. Hoping to sway sentiment in their favor, the townspeople of Fort Madison built this two-story courthouse in 1841, which cost them nearly $25,000. Much to their consternation another town was chosen, which led to more squabbling. After an intensive lobbying effort, Fort Madison became the permanent county seat in 1845. The courthouse sustained heavy damage in a 1911 fire and although the interior was rebuilt, unfortunately it lost its wonderful cupola. A classic example of Greek Revival Architecture, the Lee County Courthouse is located at 701 Avenue F.

130 (129 u)
Nauvoo, Illinois

We are looking across the river at the tiny hamlet of Nauvoo, Illinois eight miles downstream from Fort Madison. In 1839 Joseph Smith, the founding prophet of the Mormon church, whose followers had recently been expelled from Missouri, arrived at this site to establish an earthly home for his growing flock. Smith named his new Zion Nauvoo, a Hebrew word meaning "Beautiful Place."
Mormons from around the United States were attracted to this river community and by 1842 Nauvoo had become one of the largest settlements in Illinois. The Mormons started building a grand temple on a hill overlooking the Mississippi. Almost from its inception Nauvoo was subjected to a terror campaign by its non-Mormon neighbors. Their persecution culminated on June 27, 1844 when Joseph Smith and his brother Hyrum, were murdered by a mob in Carthage, Illinois. Feeling betrayed and alone, the Mormons, led by Brigham Young, decided in 1845 to abandon Nauvoo and migrate to Utah. They hastily completed work on the temple and by 1846 this community, which only one year earlier had 12,000 inhabitants was reduced to a ghost town. Nauvoo became the scene of a second bold experiment in 1849 when several hundred French immigrants called Icarians established a Utopian community here. Led by Etienne Cabet, they practiced a communal lifestyle sharing all property and possessions. Plagued by internal strife, in 1860 it was permanently dissolved. In the 1960's the Mormon church restored the city's old historic district.

FORT MADISON, IOWA.
Lee Co. Court House, Jail & Sheriff's Residence

Bird's-Eye View of Nauvoo, Ill.

131
Mansion House

Obviously in need of some repair, this two-story frame residence was the Nauvoo home of Joseph Smith, the founder of the Mormon Church. When Smith moved with his family to Nauvoo in 1839, their first home was a rudimentary log cabin. Overwhelmed finally by a need for space, Smith built this new home, which was completed in 1842. One year later Smith built an extensive wing on the rear of the house, which he operated as a hotel called the Nauvoo Mansion. After the Mormon exodus from Nauvoo, Joseph Smith's widow, Emma, took over management of the hotel and operated it successfully for just over 20 years. In 1890 the extra hotel wing was razed, and in 1918 Emma Smith's heirs deeded the original house to the Reorganized Church of Latter Day Saints. They quickly restored what was now called the Mansion House, and it became Nauvoo's first unofficial tourist attraction.

An outstanding example of period architecture, the Mansion House is now the centerpiece of the church's multi-block historic district. Without question Nauvoo's most beautiful restored home, it is located at the corner of Water and Main.

132
Brigham Young House

This unimposing brick residence, as the caption indicates, was the Nauvoo home of Brigham Young, the man who led the Mormons in their remarkable migration to Utah. Young, who was one of the church's senior apostles, moved with his family to Nauvoo in 1839. Initially they lived in a log house and in 1843 Young, who was a carpenter by trade, built this two-story brick home. In the year immediately following Joseph Smith's death in 1844 many of the church's most important decisions were made in this home, including most of the planning for the exodus to Utah. Shortly after Young left Nauvoo in 1846 the home was sold for $600 at a public auction and over the next century it passed through a number of hands before it was finally abandoned in 1951.

In the early 1960's the Young Home was the first building in Nauvoo restored by the Mormon Church. This significant historic site, which houses a number of Young family heirlooms, is situated at the corner of Granger and Kimball.

"Joseph Smith Mansion House" Nauvoo, Ill.

Brigham Young Home
Nauvoo, Ill.

133
Nauvoo House

The Nauvoo House is a poignant memorial to all the unfulfilled dreams that Joseph Smith had for his ill-fated Mormon community at Nauvoo. In 1841 Smith received a revelation to build a hotel to rival anything yet built along the Mississippi River. Construction on the hotel, which was to be a massive three-story L shaped building with two separate 120 x 40 foot wings, began in the spring of 1841. The hotel was plagued by an assortment of problems and work progressed slowly until finally in 1843 the project was abandoned. All there was to show for two years of toil was a basement and a portion of the second story frame. After the Mormon exodus from Nauvoo, Joseph Smith's widow, Emma, gained title to the property and in 1869 her second husband, Lewis Bidamon, built this two-story home on the southeast corner of the building's foundation. In 1908 the Bidamon family sold this stone structure to the Reorganized Church of Latter Day Saints.

Over the last several decades the Nauvoo House has been used as a youth hostel by the church. This impressive stone structure is located at the foot of Main Street just a few feet from the Mississippi River.

134
St. Mary's Academy

This sprawling complex of buildings and fields is the old campus of St. Mary's Academy, a renowned girl's school. In the mid-Nineteenth Century a young woman who wanted an education had a limited range of options because public schooling had yet to gain wide acceptance, and most private schools were male-only institutions. To fill this void an order of Benedictine Sisters based in Chicago opened this boarding school for girls at Nauvoo in 1874. They selected Nauvoo as a site for their school because it was a peaceful oasis with few distractions, and yet it was also close to a number of large Iowa communities. The school quickly acquired a reputation for excellence and by 1900 there were several hundred girls enrolled at St. Mary's. Although facing the same challenge that made boarding schools a nearly extinct species, St. Mary's has managed to survive and it now attracts students from all over the United States.

Nearly all of St. Mary's older buildings, including the structures pictured here, were torn down and replaced in the 1960's. A school with a proud and rich tradition, it sits on the edge of a hill at the corner of Knight and Wells.

St. Mary's Academy, Nauvoo, Ill.

135
Keokuk Monument

The Keokuk Monument is a unique testimony to a different time and different attitudes. In 1883 when Keokuk formally adopted the idea of developing a new park there was a general consensus that it should contain a monument honoring the city's namesake, Chief Keokuk. They then took things one step further by organizing an effort to have Keokuk's remains transferred from his Kansas grave and re-intern them in the park - something today which would be considered both reprehensible and unthinkable. After a minimal amount of negotiating they got their wish and in 1883 he was buried under this 30-foot high sandstone column.

In 1913 a bronze statue of Keokuk was placed atop this monument, a further tribute to an Indian leader whose name meant Watchful Fox. The monument is located near the entrance to Rand Park at 15th and Grand.

136
Keokuk Dam

By any measure the Keokuk Dam, Power Plant and Canal, seen here in this sweeping panorama, was one of the greatest engineering feats of the early Twentieth Century. The initiative for this project was provided by a group of Keokuk citizens who banded together in 1899 to study the feasibility of building a dam that would tap into the potential generating power of the Des Moines Rapids. After gaining government approval to build a private dam, the group hired Hugh Cooper, an enormously talented engineer, to design and supervise its construction. Built in just over three years at a cost of 20 million dollars, the project was completed in the summer of 1913. The dam itself, which is nearly a mile long, was at that time the largest concrete dam in the world and the facility was powered by what were the largest turbines ever built.

Even after all these years, the Keokuk Dam is still one of the country's most efficient generating stations. One of the river's most notable attractions, the power house is located at the north end of Water Street.

GENERAL VIEW OF MISSISSIPPI RIVER POWER PLANT, GOVERNMENT LOCK AND DRY DOCK. KEOKUK. IOWA. 79

137 (129 l)
C.R. Joy Home

This elegant house is representative of the houses located along Grand Avenue, Keokuk's most prestigious residential street. Grand Avenue, which sits atop a ridge immediately adjacent to the Mississippi, was a departure from the usual pattern that existed in river communities, where the wealthy were reluctant to live near the river where the heavy industry and rail lines were concentrated. That didn't happen in Keokuk, at least along this section of the river, and by the 1880's Grand Avenue had become the fashionable place to live. The street was reaching its architectural peak when Clyde Joy, a prosperous businessman, erected this house at 816 Grand. Completed in 1897, the Joy House is the street's finest example of Queen Anne architecture.

Grand Avenue has retained all of its original splendor and exclusiveness, and this island of luxurious homes is located in east central Keokuk directly south of Rand Park.

138 (130 u)
Keokuk-Hamilton Bridge

Marvelously captured in this panoramic view, the Keokuk-Hamilton Bridge is one of the oldest surviving bridges on the Upper Mississippi River. Linking the communities of Keokuk, Iowa and Hamilton, Illinois, it opened in the fall of 1870 and was the river's first dual wagon railroad bridge. Eleven years later on November 4, 1881, it was dealt a near fatal blow when the steamer War Eagle, running out of control, slammed into the structure knocking out one whole section of its span. While it was being rebuilt, the missing section was replaced by the Mississippi River's one and only covered bridge. The structure took on a new look in 1916 with the addition of a separate deck for automobiles and pedestrians.

In 1985 a new highway bridge was built just downstream connecting Keokuk and Hamilton, but this structure wasn't demolished as the railroad still needed its lower deck. What makes this bridge special today is that several years ago the City of Keokuk converted the upper deck into an observation platform, complete with benches and, yes, even a couple of picnic tables.

Residence of C. R. Joy, Keokuk, Ia.

Keokuk and Hamilton Bridge, Keokuk, Ia.

139
Hamilton

In this street scene featuring a trolley, Hamilton, Illinois looks very much like a big city metropolis. Named in honor of one of its original proprietors, Hamilton, which sits on a bluff directly opposite Keokuk, Iowa, was founded in 1852. Surrounded by rich farmland and benefiting from its link with Keokuk, the community rapidly developed into a flourishing commercial center. The town's unique enterprise was the Dadant and Sons Apiary. Founded in the 1860's by Charles Dadant, this family owned business had one of the country's largest bee colonies and was a major producer of both honey and wax.

Modern Hamilton has in many ways become an extension of neighboring Keokuk. The interurban trolley, which connected these two communities was abandoned in 1921. Most of the town's businesses are still congregated along Broadway which remains a viable commercial district.

140
Chautauqua at Hamilton

These people are enjoying breaks between shows at a Chautauqua, taking place in Hamilton, Illinois sometime around 1906. Now little more then a strange sounding word, the Chautauqua was the most anticipated event of the summer in small and medium size communities like Hamilton in the early decades of this century. Often referred to as the "Traveling Chautauqua" they were a popularized version of an adult education movement, born at Lake Chautauqua, New York in the 1870's. The Chautauqua that small town America knew was a traveling troupe of entertainers and educators who staged week-long performances inside a huge canvas tent. Audiences might see anything from a college professor lecturing on biology to a magician doing card tricks.

The Chautauqua at Hamilton was usually held the second week of August in an open field or park. And quite obviously, the local postcard publisher did his best to promote the event. Whatever their virtues, Chautauquas like the one that visited Hamilton, weren't able to compete with radio and other forms of entertainment that were coming into vogue, and by 1930 they had faded into extinction.

Broadway, Hamilton, Ill.

J.A.GORDON,

CHAUTAUQUA GROUNDS, HAMILTON, ILL.

141
Warsaw, Illinois

Humming with activity, this is what the Main Street of Warsaw, Illinois looked like back at the beginning of this century. On the shore opposite the mouth of the Des Moines River, Warsaw was founded in 1834 by a group of businessmen led by Major John Wilcox. The town grew slowly at first but by 1850 it had several sizable hotels and its riverfront had become one long column of grist mills and packing plants. In 1861 Rudolf Giller founded what would become Warsaw's most enduring and successful enterprise, the Popel and Giller Brewery. This brewery which produced a number of very popular regional beers managed to stay in business until 1972.

Nearly all of the buildings depicted in this scene have survived and the street features an eclectic mix of architectural styles. Among its more notable buildings are an 1835 hotel and distinctive Art Nouveau bank building constructed in 1920.

142
Warsaw School

Identified here as Secretary Hay's first school, this Warsaw building is one of those inconspicuous yet highly significant historic landmarks. A modest one-story brick building, this structure was built in 1835 and served as the town's first schoolhouse. One of the things that makes it notable is that John Hay, who was Secretary of State in the administration of Theodore Roosevelt, attended school here from 1848 to 1853.

One of the oldest buildings in Warsaw, this structure was last used as a school in 1903. For the past few decades it has been used as an American Legion Post and the interior has been altered quite substantially. Still a building with a lot of Nineteenth Century charm, this old schoolhouse is located at 240 North Fourth Street.

MAIN STREET WARSAW, ILL.

SECRETARY HAY'S FIRST SCHOOL
WARSAW, ILL.

143
Warsaw Button Factory

The Warsaw Button Factory is an example of the many button shops that once existed in small Upper Mississippi towns like Warsaw. Transforming mussel shells into buttons was a multi-step process that began in the small town button shops where workers machine-cut mass quantities of button blanks. The blanks were then shipped to factories in towns like Muscatine and Davenport where they were polished and had holes cut in them. Small town button shops were a risky proposition and the vast majority had a life span of less then ten years.

Somewhat larger then the typical button plant, this Warsaw facility, which opened in 1907, provided employment for about four dozen men. It certainly was a lot more successful then most of its competitors because it managed to stay in business until the late 1920's.

144
Fort Edwards Monument

This granite shaft monument marks the site of Fort Edwards from which eventually grew the town of Warsaw, Illinois. The fort was one of several military installations built along the Upper Mississippi between 1812 and 1820, whose primary purpose was to deter British traders from entering this area. Perhaps the most notable aspect of the fort, which was built sometime around 1817, was that its first commander was Major Zachary Taylor, a future U.S. President. The U.S. Army abandoned the fort in 1824 and for a few brief years it was utilized as a trading post before it eventually fell into an irreversible state of disrepair.

The citizens of Warsaw provided the lion's share of the money for this fifty-foot high granite monument, which was erected in 1914. Two decades later, Warsaw handed this memorial over to the State of Illinois. Standing atop a very prominent bluff, the monument is situated at the north end of Third Street.

Button Factory.
Warsaw, Ill.

Ft. Edward Monument, Warsaw, Ill.

145 (130 l)
LaGrange, Missouri

The rhythm of small town life is captured for us in this view looking up the Main Street in LaGrange, Missouri. Situated ten miles upstream from Quincy, Illinois, LaGrange was founded in 1832 and the majority of its first residents were transplanted southerners from Kentucky and Virginia. This community quickly blossomed into a key river landing and by 1860 its levee was a tightly packed wall of packing plants, flour mills and cooper shops. LaGrange's prosperity ended with the demise of the steamboat trade in the 1870's and because of its inability to transform itself into a railroad town. Most of its businesses gravitated to either Quincy or Hannibal leaving LaGrange essentially a backwater. The town's main claim to fame is that it was the boyhood home of Vice President Thomas R. Marshall the man who coined the phrase, "What this country needs is a really good five cent cigar."

LaGrange has also been the unfortunate victim of periodic flooding. And, as a consequence, very little of its old Main Street has survived.

146 (131 u)
Quincy Levee

Taken from the vessel in the foreground, this view allows us to experience, at least vicariously, what it must have been like to be on a steamboat that was pulling up to a river landing. I guess if you were a passenger the first thing that would catch your eye would be the building immediately adjacent to the river, which was called a wharfboat. Obviously not a boat, it was the steamboat industry's version of a train depot. All freight moving in and out of the landing was processed here and the agent inside also sold passenger tickets. The reason they were called wharfboats was that many of them were fashioned out of old steamboat hulls.

The wharfboats real heyday was between 1840 and 1870, and by 1920 nearly all of them had been either razed or converted into warehouses. This wharfboat, which was built by the Diamond Jo Packet Company, had a bit longer run before it was finally razed sometime around 1930.

MAIN ST. N. LA GRANGE, MO.

Boat Landing, Quincy, Ill.

147 (131 l)
Washington Park

This summertime scene captures the intrinsic appeal of Washington Park, which throughout the years has been the prototypical town square. Born out of a desire to provide a well-defined center for a community and as a public refuge and gathering place, the town square was a result of New England ingenuity. Washington Park was established in the 1820's and very quickly many of the town's leading commercial enterprises coalesced around it. The park gained national attention when it was the site of the sixth Lincoln-Douglas Debate held on October 13, 1858 with 13,000 people in attendance. Over the last three decades of the Nineteenth Century it acquired all the features commonly associated with a town square, including this fountain and bandstand. Unlike most towns, Quincy had managed to preserve the integrity of its town square. The park contains updated versions of its old fountain and bandstand along with several historic gems including a statue of the town's founder, John Wood, and a placque commemorating the Lincoln-Douglas Debate. Immaculately maintained, Washington Park is bounded by Fourth, Fifth, Maine and Hampshire.

148 (132 u)
John Wood Mansion

This distinguished house museum was built by a man of great accomplishment and vision, John Wood, Quincy's first settler. Wood was a young man of twenty-four when he established the town of Quincy in 1822. By prudent real estate investing, he quickly amassed a sizable fortune and in 1835 built this imposing Greek Revival home. Wood then entered the political arena and was a fourth term mayor before becoming the 12th Governor of Illinois in 1860. Although well into his sixties, Wood served with distinction in the Civil War and then lived out his remaining years in this house, where he died in 1880.

In 1907 the John Wood House was purchased by the Historical Society of Quincy which spent over $400,000 restoring this important landmark. Built in the style of a southern mansion, this fourteen-room house museum is furnished with many items that belonged to the Wood family, along with a fine selection of antiques. This old and ornate structure is located at 425 S. 12th Street.

Fountain and Band Stand,
Union Park, Quincy, Ill.

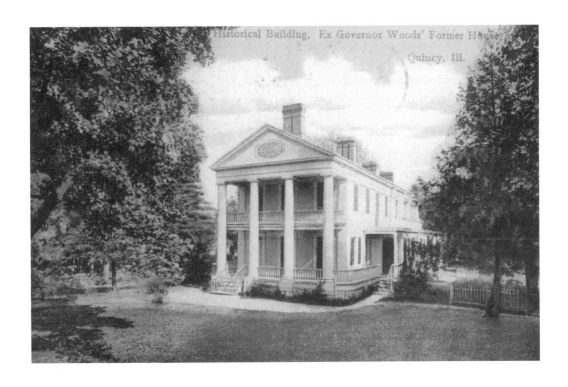

Historical Building, Ex Governor Woods' Former House,
Quincy, Ill.

149 (132 l)
Villa Katherine

This peculiar looking building is the Mississippi Valley's one and only example of Moorish architecture, and as you might expect the man who built it was an eccentric character named George Metz. A native of Quincy, Metz inherited a vast fortune from his parents in the 1890's, and rather than work he decided to go on a world tour. While in North Africa, Metz became intrigued with Moorish castles and decided, upon his return, to build one in Quincy. It was completed in 1900 and he named this structure the Villa Katherine, in honor of his mother. For the next twelve years Metz lived the life of a recluse with his sole companion, a two-hundred pound Great Dane who slept on a Turkish rug. In 1912 Metz sold the Villa Katherine and spent the remaining twenty-five years of his life ensconced in a Quincy hotel room.

After Metz sold the Villa Katherine it passed through a number of hands and was used for everything from a rec center to a rooming house. In an effort to preserve its heritage, Quincy rehabilitated this structure in the 1980's, and it now houses a tourist information center. The Villa Katherine is located at 532 Gardner Expressway.

150
Steamboat Traveling Past Hannibal, Missouri

All the awe and mystique of steamboating are beautifully captured in this timeless scene of an unidentified boat, pushing several barges loaded with freight, cruising past Hannibal, Missouri. Regrettably, in the first decade of this century, scenes like this one were atypical because railroad companies like the Illinois Central and Rock Island had long ago displaced the steamboat and were exercising a monopolistic stronghold on freight transportation in the Upper Mississippi Valley. Generally speaking, the few steamers that were hauling cargo during this era were smaller boats, making short trips of 20 to 100 miles and loaded with items running the gamut from apples to clam shells. The rebirth of river commerce along this waterway began in the early 1920's. There were many factors that contributed to this rebirth but the biggest single reason was that the railroads had so abused their monopolistic pricing power that it was once again economically viable for water carriers to transport freight.

Villa Kathrine, Quincy, Ill.

Steamboat and Barges going up the Mississippi River, Hannibal, Mo.

151 (133 u)
Mark Twain Statue

This statue is Hannibal, Missouri's official monument to its most famous resident. Situated on the edge of a 300-foot bluff in Riverview Park, this statue was unveiled in 1913. Depicting Twain as he looked in his seventies, it was sculpted by Frederick Hibbard and paid for by the State of Missouri. The inscription on the statue's base is a touching testimony to this great man: "His religion was humanity and a whole world mourned for him when he died."
Encompassing approximately 400 acres, Riverview Park is located one mile south of downtown Hannibal.

152 (133 l)
Mark Twain Boyhood Home

The Mark Twain Boyhood Home is the one landmark most often associated with the Mississippi River. Surprisingly we can't say exactly when this famous structure was built and all we are sure of is that it was erected sometime in the early 1840's. The record is clear that in 1844 John Marshall Clemens, his wife Jane, and their six children occupied this unpretentious house. When they moved into their new home Samuel Clemens was nine years old. Except for a brief period following the death of John Clemens in 1847 the Clemens family lived in this house until 1853 when they left Hannibal and headed upriver to Iowa.
In the years following their departure, this home became part of a less than desirable district. It was surrounded by foul-smelling industrial plants and further handicapped by its close proximity to the town's rail line. From at least 1870 onward the Twain Home was a low rent property and there were often two families living in this small six-room residence. The house gained its first measure of fame when Samuel Clemens posed for a photograph in front of his old home in 1902. This structure became a butcher shop in 1911 and there was talk circulating that it was about to be torn down. Hannibal mobilized to preserve this landmark and on the town's behalf Mr. and Mrs. George Mahan purchased the house. The Mahans restored the house and then presented it to the city at a gala public ceremony held on May 15, 1912. The Mark Twain Boyhood Home was already becoming a national shrine when a museum was built alongside it in 1937. Over the last 60 years an estimated eight million people have toured this white clapboard home. This landmark is situated two blocks west of the river at 202 Hill Street.

Mark Twain Monument,
Riverview Park, Hannibal, Mo.

Mark Twain's Home, Hannibal, Mo.

153 (134 u)
Huck Finn House

This rather forlorn looking Hannibal residence was in a manner of speaking the home of Huckleberry Finn. It was the boyhood home of Tom Blankenship, who provided the model for Samuel Clemens' Huck Finn. We don't have a lot of biographical information on Mr. Blankenship, but by all accounts he was hardly a model citizen. One of eight children, Blankenship had several brushes with the law both as teenager and adult, and he was once caught stealing a shirt from a Hannibal store. Blankenship's association with Hannibal ended in the mid-1860's when he moved to some unspecified location out west and was never heard from again.

The Blankenship family resided in this home, which was located a block west of the Mark Twain Boyhood Home, from about 1830 to 1850. Always considered an eyesore, it was badly damaged in a 1903 fire and then finally razed sometime around 1910.

154 (134 l)
Rockcliffe Mansion

More than just a palatial residence, this Hannibal mansion was the ultimate reflection of the wealth created by lumbering along the Upper Mississippi in the Nineteenth Century. One of the characteristics of the lumber barons from that era was an almost compulsive need to own the showiest residence in the community. One man outdid them all, John J. Cruikshank, Hannibal's most successful lumbering magnate. A man who settled only for the best, Cruikshank poured much of his wealth into this 30-room Georgian style showplace, which took three years to build and was completed in 1900. Beyond its sheer massiveness, the mansion had many opulent appointments, including 10 carved marble and tile fireplaces, walk-in closets, and a grand staircase.

The Cruikshank family vacated this mansion in 1924 and it stood empty for 43 years, and then in the late 1960's it was painstakingly restored to its original condition by several local residents. This famous house museum sits atop one of Hannibal's highest hills at 1000 Bird Street.

Home of Huckleberry Finn, Hannibal, Mo.

P-26608

CRUIKSHANK RESIDENCE, HANNIBAL, MO.

155 (135 u)
Lover's Leap

This gentleman is pondering the view from Lover's Leap, a lofty bluff at the south end of Hannibal. The bluff draws its name from a story concocted by Sam Clemens' older brother Orion. In 1840 he published an article in the Hannibal paper recounting a supposed Indian tale about a princess and a brave from different tribes who became lovers. When their parents refused to let them marry the couple jumped from the top of this ledge, plunging to their death. No one realized that Orion had fabricated the whole story and from that point onward this bluff has been called Lover's Leap.

Offering a panoramic view of Hannibal, this 250-foot high bluff now has an observation platform. The entrance to Lover's Leap is located one-half mile south of Hannibal on Highway 79.

156
Mark Twain Cave

We are looking at the entrance to a cave which will forever be remembered as the dark labyrinth where Tom Sawyer and Becky Thatcher became so hopelessly lost in *The Adventures of Tom Sawyer*. This cave has a rich history dating back almost to the founding of Hannibal. Jack Simms, who was one of the town's initial settlers, accidentally stumbled upon the cave in 1819 when he and his dog were exploring the area. In the decades that followed, the cave was used as a storeroom for firearms, a private mausoleum, possibly a stop on the underground railroad and, of course, a place that every Hannibal youngster loved to explore. Shortly after the publication of *The Adventures of Tom Sawyer* in 1876 the owner of the property opened it to the public (at a charge) and it is therefore one of the Midwest's oldest tourists attractions.

What is particularly notable about this venerable old cave is that its walls are decorated with graffiti dating all the way back to the 1820's. Designated a United States National Landmark in 1972, the Mark Twain Cave is located two miles south of Hannibal.

1759
Mark Twain
Cave,
Hannibal, Mo.

199

157
Louisiana, Missouri

This section of West Georgia Street contains some of the most fashionable homes in Louisiana, Missouri. Situated 28 miles downstream from Hannibal, Missouri, Louisiana was founded in 1818 by two former Kentucky residents, Joel Shaw and Samuel Caldwell. It was little more than a trading post but by the 1840's it had developed into a flour milling center. Beginning in the 1870's the town's economy shifted its focus to tobacco. In the last three decades of the Nineteenth Century tobacco was the leading cash crop in northeast Missouri and Louisiana was the processing and marketing center for this profitable commodity. At one point in the 1890's there were 14 tobacco plants in Louisiana. Unable to compete in a marketplace increasingly dominated by corporate giants like the American Tobacco Company, most of these firms went out of business shortly after the turn of the century.

Most of the elegant homes along this tree-lined boulevard were built between 1870 and 1900. Architecturally many have a decidedly Southern look because many of the town's leading citizens of that era were from Virginia and South Carolina.

158
Fargo and Phelps Shoe Factory – Louisiana Missouri

This Louisiana, Missouri shoe factory symbolized the highly localized nature of manufacturing and industry along the Upper Mississippi in the early years of this century. At this time it wasn't all that unusual for even a mid-size community like Louisiana to have its own shoe factory, furniture plant or even a brewery. And often many of these companies were able to sell their products to distributors in big city markets.

The Fargo and Phelps Shoe Company moved into this plant in 1907 and a decade later won a major contract from the U.S. Army to manufacture infantry boots. After the war the company fell on hard times and in 1925 a glove manufacturer moved into the plant. Today the plant, which is located at 600 South Main, houses a company which makes electrical conduit pipes.

COPYRIGHT 1910 CATLETT.

West Georgia Street,
looking West,
Louisiana, Mo.

Barge & Phelps Shoe Factory,
Louisiana, Mo.

159
Stark Nursery

One couldn't guess it from this postcard, but the Stark Nursery had already carved out a niche as the nation's largest and most innovative nursery. The company was founded by James Stark, a young man of 24, who arrived at this vicinity from Kentucky in 1816, carrying in his saddlebags a bundle of apple graftings that after a successful planting became one of Missouri's first apple orchards. Stark and his descendants proved to be masters of both business and horticulture and by the 1870's the company was universally recognized for producing the best fruit trees. The company's crowning achievement was the development in 1893 of the Red Delicious apple, which remains to this day America's most popular apple.

Now called the Stark Brothers Nurseries and Orchards Company, it is located about a mile west of Louisiana. The building shown here served as the corporate office from the 1880's until it was demolished in the early 1980's. One tie to the company's history that has been preserved is the log cabin home James Stark built next to his orchard in 1816.

160
Clarksville, Missouri

Hardly the picture of prosperity, this street was once the main thoroughfare in Clarksville, Missouri. One of the oldest towns on the river, Clarksville was founded in 1818 and named in honor of explorer William Clark. An early steamboat landing by 1850, the town had matured into a diversified commercial center with a number of mills. Clarksville's most famous business was the Missouri Vinegar Manufacture Works. Founded in 1866, the company was for many years the largest vinegar factory in the midwest. Handicapped because it didn't have any nearby neighbors and unable to cope with decline in river traffic, Clarksville by 1900 had been reduced to an insignificant railroad stop.

When a new highway was built through Clarksville in the 1960's, the commercial strip, which adjoins the river, was all but abandoned. The highway however enabled Clarksville to grow into a tourist haven and in the 1980's a developer rehabilitated the entire block in the left corner of this scene.

STARK NURSERY OFFICE, LA. MO.

Main Street, Clarksville, Mo.

161
Grafton

This bird's eye view of Grafton, Illinois was taken from a bluff at the east end of town. Positioned just below the mouth of the Illinois River, Grafton was platted in 1836 by Sarah Mason. The hills surrounding Grafton once contained some of the finest limestone deposits in the Mississippi Valley and by the 1850's quarrying had become the mainstay of this town's economy. Grafton stone was used on a number of major building projects including the river's most famous span, the Eads Bridge. Late in the Nineteenth Century this community also became an important boat-building center.

Stone is no longer quarried here but Grafton still remains wedded to the river and many of its residents are employed in the barge industry. Like many of its neighbors, Grafton has reaped the benefits of tourism and many of its old buildings now house gift shops and guest cottages.

162
Elsah

Neatly nestled in a small valley adjoining the river five miles downstream from Grafton, Illinois, Elsah was founded in 1853 by James Semple. During its first two decades the town prospered as a shipping point for grain and among its businesses were several flour mills and distilleries. Elsah's growth was stifled by its relative isolation and after a failed attempt to become a resort community in the 1890's its economy collapsed.

New life was pumped into Elsah in the 1930's when Principia College transferred its campus to a bluff overlooking this Nineteenth Century river hamlet. The town's renewal was given further impetus with the completion of the McAdams Highway in 1965. Widely acclaimed as one of the best preserved towns in the midwest, in 1973 this entire community was placed on the National Register of Historic Places.

Looking West From Quarry Bluff, Grafton, Ill.　　　703　C. U. WILLIAMS, PHOTOETTE, BLOOMINGTON, ILL.

Main Street, Elsah, Ills.

163
Portage Des Sioux, Missouri

This meager looking collection of buildings represented what was once the commercial district of Portage Des Sioux, Missouri. Situated five miles upstream from Alton, Illinois this old river settlement was founded in 1799 by Francis LeSieur. He named it Portage Des Sioux as it was at the head of a portage that was used by the Sioux Indians. Starting out as a trading post, the town's one brush with history occurred in 1816 when a peace treaty was negotiated here between representatives of the United States government and a confederation of Indian tribes. Despite its early founding, Portage Des Sioux never developed into anything more than a tiny fishing village.

It's a marvel that Portage Des Sioux has survived because its proximity to the Missouri River and the mouth of the Illinois River makes it very susceptible to flooding. On more than one occasion it has been completely inundated by floodwaters but its plucky inhabitants have refused to abandon this community. Flooding has erased all traces of the town's old commercial district.

164
Bluff Line

We are looking north in this view along the tracks of the Bluff Line Railroad which once ran between Grafton and Alton, Illinois. A feeder line of the Chicago, Peoria and St. Louis Railroad completed in 1890, the Bluff Line ushered in a new era for the communities along this route. Prior to this date, their only access to the outside world was by boat, and now with a rail line, tourists and sightseers started streaming into this small corridor. Resort hotels and summer cottages sprang up to accommodate this influx, which unfortunately was short-lived, and by 1915 the area had regressed to the status of a backwater.

One might say history is repeating itself. A modern expressway called the McAdams Highway was completed along the route of the old Bluff Line in 1965. Once again tourists are being drawn back to this scenic corridor, which has the makings this time of a permanent community.

MAIN STREET, PORTAGE DES SIOUX, MO.

Scene along the Bluff Line, near Alton, Ill.

165 (135 l)
Lovejoy Monument

Conveying a sense of hope and triumph, this Alton Monument is a memorial to Elijah P. Lovejoy, a man who sacrificed his life in the cause of freedom. A Presbyterian Minister, Reverend Lovejoy migrated to Alton in 1836 and immediately began publishing a stridently anti-slavery newspaper. The newspaper inflamed passions in a town deeply divided on the slavery issue, and those who favored slavery waged a fierce campaign to silence Lovejoy. Finally on the night of November 9, 1837 things came to a head when an angry mob stormed a warehouse where Lovejoy and some of his supporters were guarding a recently acquired printing press. In the ensuing struggle, Reverend Lovejoy was killed and the printing press was thrown into the river. His death was not in vain, as it helped swell the ranks of those openly opposed to slavery.

The monument, which is a 93-foot granite shaft surmounted by a statue of the Roman Goddess of Victory, was unveiled on November 9, 1897, the 60th anniversary of Lovejoy's death. Honoring the spirit of a great American, it stands at the entrance to the Alton Cemetery at Fifth and Monument.

166 (136 u)
St. Peter and St. Paul Cathedral

When this picture was taken Sts. Peter and Paul's Cathedral was perhaps the most important building in Alton. The town's second Catholic Church, it was built in 1855 under the direction of Reverend Michael Carroll. Providence smiled on this edifice almost immediately because in 1857 the Catholic hierarchy made Alton a see and the church became a Cathedral. The state's population base slowly began shifting to the east and finally it was decided in 1923 to transfer the see from Alton to Springfield, and this once again became a parish church.

The only significant change to this Gothic style church occurred several decades ago when the original steeple had to be replaced after it was hit by a bolt of lightening. Just to the right of the church in this view is the Bishop's Residence built in 1859, which is also a notable and well preserved landmark. These two cherished church structures are located on the crest of a hill at 721 State Street.

Lovejoy Monument, Alton, Ill.

3606. St. Peter and St. Paul's Cathedral, Bishop's Residence and School, Alton, Ill.

167
Alton Prison

Hardly more then a pile of rubble, this is the last surviving remnant of the infamous Alton Prison. When the tide of battle in the Civil War began shifting in favor of the Union Army, one of the chief concerns became where to house all the prisoners they were receiving. There really wasn't a coherent plan to cope with the problem and most temporary camps like the Alton Prison were unfit for human habitation. This facility was an old state penitentiary dating from 1833 that had been abandoned in 1860 because its condition was so deplorable. The first prisoners began arriving at this cramped and outdated prison in 1862, and almost immediately a smallpox epidemic broke out. Repeated attempts were made to stop this dreadful scourge but it ran unchecked for nearly two years, claiming the lives of over 1,000 helpless men.

After the war ended, the Alton Prison was demolished and although most of its stones were carted away for building material, the city did manage to preserve this one small section of its outer wall. Part of the Civil War's darker side, this memorial is located near the intersection of Broadway and William.

168
Standard Oil Plant

A harbinger of the new industrial era, this Standard Oil facility was the Upper Mississippi Valley's first oil refinery. After exploring a number of potential sites in the St. Louis area officials of the Standard Oil Company decided in 1906 to build a refinery on farmland adjacent to the river four miles south of Alton, Illinois. They chose this location because the land was inexpensive, it offered access to several rail lines and it was just a short distance from one of the country's largest and fastest growing markets. Named the Wood River Refinery, this complex was completed in 1907 and most of its workers lived in the community that grew up alongside Wood River, Illinois. The success of this refinery drew other oil companies to the area and by the 1920's the east bank of the river between Alton and East St. Louis had become thickly packed with refineries and chemical plants.

Amoco, Standard Oil's corporate successor, closed this refinery in 1981. The industrial legacy it helped create remains very much intact because this section of the river is still the exclusive domain of giant oil and chemical concerns.

Ruins of Old Penitentiary, Alton, Ill.

860 View of Standard Oil Plant, near Alton, Ill. 1917

169 (136 l)
Water Intake Tower Number One

From a casual glance one could almost conclude that we're looking here at a medieval castle popping out of the water, but in reality is it one of St. Louis' unique and historic water intake towers. Just downstream from the mouth of the Missouri, this structure was erected in 1894 to draw water from the river and funnel it into the city's water system. Built with a sense of style, the tower, which is 92-feet high, rests on a foundation of granite blocks. Those who manned this facility traveled back and forth on a dike which is now submerged.

In 1915 a second and equally impressive intake tower was built a few hundred feet to the east of this river landmark. The best vista, other than the river, for viewing these twin towers is Chain of Rocks Park, which is located at the northern tip of St. Louis.

170 (137 u)
Eads Bridge

Viewed here from the foot of Washington Avenue, the Eads Bridge heralded a new era for St. Louis, and it remains to this day one of the world's great bridges. The first bridge to span the river at St. Louis, the structure is named for the man who designed and supervised its construction, James B. Eads. His imaginative plan broke new ground in a number of areas including the coupling of piers, raising steel arch tubing and sinking both the abutments and piers to depths never before attempted. Because so much of the work had to be done underwater, it took nearly six and a half years to build this 1,700 foot long bridge, which was completed in the summer of 1874.

The bridge's durability has surpassed even Eads' most optimistic expectation, having survived a direct hit by a tornado in 1896. Further proof of its durability was demonstrated in the Fall of 1993 when its old rail deck was incorporated into the area's new Metro Link rapid transit system. Easily the Mississippi's most venerable bridge, this mammoth structure spans the river just north of the Gateway Arch.

12331. Intake Tower, Water Works, Chain of Rocks, St. Louis, Mo.

EADS BRIDGE, ST. LOUIS, MO.

171
St. Louis Levee

The sorrowful state of steamboating at the turn of the century is dramatically reflected in this scene of a St. Louis levee almost devoid of any activity. By contrast, in the mid-Nineteenth Century during the steamboat's golden era, this same wharf was a boisterous and lively avenue crammed with dozens of arriving and departing boats. The levee itself, nearly three miles of river front, was usually covered with a blanket of cargo coming from or heading for nearby warehouses.

This levee, with all its many memories, became a complete anachronism with the introduction in the 1920's of a single river terminal. It was perhaps only fitting that the last surviving section of the levee between Washington and Poplar was razed in the 1930's and incorporated into what would become the Jefferson National Expansion Memorial.

172
Old Cathedral

Affectionately known as the Old Cathedral, this stone edifice is the last surviving link to the days when St. Louis was a frontier outpost. Situated a few paces from the site of the city's first Catholic church built in 1770, this historic Cathedral was consecrated on October 26, 1834. A beacon of hope and refuge for newly arriving immigrants, the Old Cathedral was one of only a handful of buildings in the river front district to survive the Great Fire of 1849, which began on a steamer. Fortune smiled on it again in the 1930's when it was the only building spared in a forty-block demolition in preparation for the Gateway Arch.

The Old Cathedral is constructed of limestone and its exterior is dominated by a massive forty-foot wide portico. The sanctuary contains a number of priceless treasures, including a painting of St. Louis IX, given as a gift to the Bishop of St. Louis by the King of France in 1818. One of the premier historic landmarks in the Upper Mississippi Valley, the Old Cathedral today quietly reposes near the south base of the Gateway Arch.

Old Cathedral (Catholic) St. Louis. U. S. A.

173
Old Courthouse

Shown here dwarfed a newly completed cluster of skyscrapers, this structure, which is now called the Old Courthouse, had been the landmark of downtown St. Louis for well over a century. Hampered by a series of delays, it took twenty-three years to construct this Greek Revival Style building, which was finally completed in 1862. The Courthouse's most arresting architectural feature is its rotunda, that has four galleries which are supported by a stately assemblage of Ionic and Corinthian columns. Historically the Courthouse is significant because it was the scene of a number of eventful public gatherings in the Nineteenth Century, and also because it was the setting for the initial phase of the famous Dred Scott Case.

In 1940 the Old Courthouse was transferred to the National Park Service, who did a wonderful job of reclaiming this historic building. The Old Courthouse, which is located at the corner of Fourth and Market, today houses a broad range of exhibits which trace this city's colorful past.

174 (137 l)
St. Louis City Hall

This view of St. Louis' City Hall doesn't capture the full expression of its commanding presence. In the late 1880's nearly everyone had conceded that St. Louis needed a new city hall, and there was an equally strong consensus that it had to be the best in the country. One could make a persuasive argument that they achieved their objective. Completed in 1904, the structure, which was patterned after the city hall of Paris, is a splendid example of French Renaissance architecture. Its exterior is decorated with a series of projecting pavilions and high topped roofs, but the building's most acclaimed feature is its four-story atrium, which has a unique divided staircase.

With the exception of the removal of its central tower in 1936, it has survived almost intact. A most under-appreciated landmark, the St. Louis City Hall is located at the intersection of Market and Tucker Boulevard.

Court House, St. Louis, Mo.

7985. City Hall, St. Louis, Mo.

175 (138 u)
Union Station

Captured here in all of its majestic glory, Union Station has often been called the "Grandest of the Grand Railway Stations" and deservedly so. Replacing a depot built in the 1870's, this railroad palace was financed by a consortium of six rail carriers. Meant to serve as a symbol of civic pride, Union Station, designed as a version of a French Chateau, opened September 1, 1894. Without question its most compelling feature is its 8,500 square foot Grand Hall, whose centerpiece is a magnificent allegorical stained glass window depicting goddesses representing St. Louis, New York and San Francisco.

Serving as the gateway to St. Louis and all points west, Union Station was one of the country's busiest depots in the 1920's with some 250 trains arriving and departing daily. However, not even this grand palace could withstand the irresistible competition from the automobile and airplane, and its days as a depot ended on October 31, 1978. Thanks to a public private partnership and an infusion of 135 million dollars, this proud edifice was successfully transformed into a shopping complex and luxury hotel in 1985. Once again the destination for travelers from around the globe, Union Station is located at the western edge of downtown at 18th and Market.

176 (138 l)
Statue of St. Louis

This gigantic bronze statue, which honors the man for whom St. Louis is named, King St. Louis IX, was until the completion of the Gateway Arch the city's most enduring and recognizable symbol. St. Louis, the most famous of Europe's "Crusader Kings" who died while leading a crusade, reigned as the King of France from 1220 to 1270. Originally cast in plaster and built expressly for the Louisiana Purchase Exposition, the figure was sculpted by Charles H. Niehaus. His work, which stood near the Exposition's entrance, became so popular an attraction that it was decided at the Fair's conclusion to have it recast in bronze and placed on permanent display in Forest Park.

The statue depicts the King galloping into battle wearing a crown and holding in his right hand a sword. The statue, which has been featured on the cover of countless books, sits majestically atop Art Hill in front of the St. Louis Art Museum.

UNION STATION, ST. LOUIS, MO.

TOTAL DIMENSIONS, 820.606 FEET
COVERING 11 ACRES

Bronze Statue of St. Louis A.T Hill-Forest Park, St. Louis, U. S. A.

177 (139 u)
Vandeventer Place

Here is a panorama of Vandeventer Place, which was at the turn of the century St. Louis' most exclusive and prestigious private street. Once a distinguishing characteristic of this great metropolis, the private street was a way for the ultra rich to shield themselves from the unsettling aspects of urban life. Onerous deed restrictions ensured the exclusiveness of these enclaves and most like Vandeventer possessed a tree-lined boulevard and a regal entrance gate. Vandeventer Place became the city's most fashionable address in the 1870's and was located just a few blocks north of St. Louis University.

Vandeventer Place gradually lost its appeal for the rich as the neighborhoods surrounding it became commercialized and regrettably all of the homes along this once famous street were razed in the 1950's. There are however a number of private streets within the confines of St. Louis that have survived almost intact.

178
Missouri Botanical Garden

These people are enjoying the lush greenery of the enchantingly beautiful Missouri Botanical Garden. This unique St. Louis treasure dates all the way back to 1851 when Henry Shaw, a wealthy businessman, decided to convert his country estate into a formal garden. Guided by a professional botanist, Shaw soon had one of the country's greatest gardens, and in 1859 he opened it to the public. Shaw spent the remainder of his life expanding and improving the garden, whose initial attractions were a herbarium and pleasure garden, and when he died in 1889 it had become a highly respected research and educational facility.

While the Missouri Botanical Garden has kept pace with the times, adding for example the world's first geodesic dome greenhouse in 1960, it has managed to retain much of its original Victorian charm and appeal. America's oldest botanical garden, this seventy-nine acre floral showplace is located in the southwest corner of the city at 4344 Shaw Boulevard.

Vandeventer Place, St. Louis, Mo.

Lily Pond, Shaw's Garden, ST. LOUIS, U. S. A.

179 (139 1)
Anheuser Busch Brewery

Looking at this sprawling complex of buildings its easy to see that even back in 1900 Anheuser Busch Brewing was the one business most often identified with the City of St. Louis. The origins of this colossus date back to 1857 when Eberhard Anheuser, a soap manufacturer, became the unwilling owner through foreclosure of a small brewery with very bleak prospects. Acting out of expediency, Anheuser made a providential move when he appointed his son-in-law, Adolphus Busch, to manage the brewery. A German immigrant who possessed an uncommon will to succeed, Busch took a small struggling company and transformed it into the nation's premier beer maker.

Most of the structures depicted in this dazzling panorama, which were built during the brewery's most dynamic years of growth between 1870 and 1900, have survived, including the Brew House, which is just to the right of the building with the twin towers. Sprawled out over 100 acres, the Anheuser Busch Brewery Plant is situated just a few blocks west of the river where Broadway and Arsenal intersect.

180
Granite City, Illinois

This unusual pairing of a train station and the mammoth National Enameling Work Plant is a telling reflection of the unique historic character of Granite City, Illinois. Situated almost equidistant between Alton and East St. Louis, Granite City is a living testimonial to the entrepreneurial genius of two German immigrants, William and Frederick Niedringhaus. Owners of an enormously successful enterprise that manufactured kitchen utensils, they made the bold decision in 1892 to transfer their operation from St. Louis to the Illinois side of the river and build a company town. Purchasing a 3,500 acre tract of land, they erected two huge manufacturing facilities, planted over 14,000 trees and built a million dollar levee to protect their new town.

It only took Granite City a decade to grow from a company town to a community with a diversified industrial base, and after a hundred years its economy still revolves around manufacturing. One of the first structures built here by the Niedringhaus brothers, the National Enameling Work Plant, now used primarily as a warehousing facility, is located at 1100 Niedringhaus Avenue. Built around 1900, the town station is now an apartment building.

A GROUP OF THE PRINCIPAL BUILDINGS
ANHEUSER-BUSCH BREWING PLANT
ST. LOUIS

Union Depot and National Enameling Works,
Granite City, Ill.

181
Flood at East St. Louis

The awesome power of a Mississippi River flood is dramatically shown in this scene of devastation at East St. Louis, Illinois during the Great Flood of 1903. Flooding had been a persistent problem at East St. Louis because the town sits near the center of the river's largest and longest floodplain. The town was protected by a ten-mile dike but it afforded only minimal protection against a major flood. Fed by unending rains upriver in late spring the Mississippi was a bloated monster when it reached floodstage here on June 1, 1903. Residents fought to reinforce their crumbling dike with sandbags, but they were overmatched by a river that wouldn't stop rising. Finally, on June 10, the main section of the dike collapsed and a torrent of water surged into the town. The flood left in its wake a severely crippled town. Hundreds of homes had to be abandoned and scores of businesses never reopened. The flood created a cycle of poverty that East St. Louis still strives to overcome.

182
Monks Mound

Although nearly all of the information in the caption is incorrect, the card itself demonstrates that Monks Mound had already acquired a national reputation, because it is the largest earthen mound in the United States. When the first settlers arrived in the area of St. Louis they found a landscape studded with hundreds of mounds and this is why for the better part of a hundred years St. Louis was called the "Mound City." St. Louis' mounds quickly fell prey to urbanization, but those across the river in Illinois, which were grouped around Monks Mound, were spared destruction because it was so sparsely settled in the Nineteenth Century. Early in that century a group of Trappist Monks had a monastery at the base of this structure and from that point on it was called Monks Mound. Archaeologists began penetrating the secrets of these mounds in the early 1920's and in 1926 the State of Illinois gained title to the land on which they were built. We now know that Monks Mound was the focal point of a sprawling metropolis which was populated by upwards of 40,000 people from 700 A.D. to 1500 A.D. Covering fourteen acres and rising to a height of 100 feet, Monks Mound was where the priestly ruler of this community resided in a temple on its summit. Part of the Cahokia Mounds World Heritage Site, this great structure is located in Collinsville, Illinois at the junction of Collinsville Road and Sun Prairie Lane.

Relay Station During High Water, East St. Louis, Ill.

Cahokia-Temple Mound, Near East St. Louis, Ill.
The largest pyramid in the world, 1080 feet long, 780 feet wide, 102 feet high. Erected by hand over 2,000 years ago, at a time when all appliances were crude and by a class of people whose life was dedicated to the most rigorous religious observances and pursuits.

183
Cahokia Courthouse

The Cahokia Courthouse is the oldest surviving building on the Upper Mississippi River and a reminder of a time when Cahokia was the most important settlement on the river. The founding of Cahokia dates back to the spring of 1699 when a group of Jesuit priests established a mission to work with the Tamaroa Indians on the east bank of the river opposite what would one day become St. Louis. Their mission soon became the site of a pathetic little French village which in 1723 had 12 inhabitants. While it may not have looked like much, Cahokia was the first permanent European settlement on the entire Mississippi River.

It soon began to attract an itinerant group of fur traders, merchants, and fortune hunters, and by 1750 had become a vital outpost in France's colonial empire. Any hopes Cahokia had of developing into anything more then a sleepy village ended in 1763 when France was forced to cede all its territory east of the Mississippi to Britain. Rather than be British subjects many of its residents relocated across the river and took up residence in St. Louis. Cahokia experienced a brief renewal under American rule but it was never destined to be anything more than a historical footnote.

Originally a private dwelling, the Cahokia Courthouse was built sometime around 1737 by Captain Jean Baptiste Saucier. His son, Francois, lived in it for many years and than in 1793 became the new courthouse for St. Clair County. Housing a jail, courtroom, and two offices, it served as a courthouse until 1814 when the county seat was transferred to Belleville.

Around 1900 this badly dilapidated structure was rediscovered and four years later it was dismantled and reassembled as an exhibit at the St. Louis World's Fair. Following the fair it was purchased by the Chicago Historical Society and placed in a Chicago park. After long years of discussion it was decided in the mid-1930's to return this famous structure to Cahokia. Meticulously rebuilt on its original stone foundation, the Cahokia Courthouse was rededicated as an Illinois historic site in the spring of 1940.

A near perfect example of French Colonial Architecture, this structure now houses exhibits relating to the early history of Cahokia. This landmark is located near the center of Cahokia at 112 Main Street.

OLD CAHOKA COURT HOUSE, FIRST COURT HOUSE IN ILLINOIS, NEAR ST. LOUIS, MO.

184
U.S. Lily

The Lily, which was probably taking on supplies when this picture was taken, belonged to the U.S. Lighthouse Service, but it had nothing whatsoever to do with lighthouses. It patrolled the Upper Mississippi installing and maintaining the thousands of oil lamps hung on wing dams that provided a beacon for pilots traveling at night. Lighthouse tenders like the Lily played a vital role on the river for a number of decades, but their importance diminished when boats started using search lights and channel markers were installed along the river. And the vast majority of the upper river's wing dams perished when the U.S. Corp. of Engineers created a new system of dams in the 1930's.

Christened in 1875, the Lily originally operated on the Ohio River and in 1890 it was reassigned to the Upper Mississippi. This medium-sized steamer became one of the river's many victims when it hit a snag and sank in the fall of 1911.

STEAMER LILY- U.S. LIGHTHOUSE TENDER-MISSISSIPPI RIVER

185
Pittsburgh Plate Glass Company

For almost a century this Crystal City, Missouri complex was one of the largest glass-making facilities in the world. Its origins date back to the fall of 1868 when a trio of scientists discovered that the sand deposits here were ideally suited for making plate glass. Four years later a small glass furnace was built, but the operation failed, and in 1876 the Crystal City Glass Company gained title to the property and remade it into a major industrial complex. They created a company town, building homes for their employees, and after a decade of rapid expansion they built a feeder line railroad. In 1895 this profitable concern was purchased by the Pittsburgh Plate Glass Company, and in 1908 they upgraded and modernized the entire facility.

This plant was the flagship factory for the Pittsburgh Plate Glass Company for well over half a century, but in the 1960's they began downsizing here when float glass began to displace plate glass. In 1991 they closed what was left of the complex and shortly thereafter all of its buildings were razed.

PITTSBURG PLATE GLASS CO.,
(LARGEST IN THE WORLD),
CRYSTAL CITY, MO.

Ste. Genevieve

We are looking down the main commercial artery of Ste. Genevieve, Missouri, the oldest permanent settlement on the west bank of the Mississippi River. This tradition rich French settlement is located sixty-five miles downstream from St. Louis, which it predates by at least a quarter of a century. In the 1720's French colonists began searching this section of the Mississippi Valley in a quest for gold or silver. They weren't nearly so lucky but they did find a rich deposit of lead in the hills adjoining a natural river landing. Sometime between 1725 and 1740 a group of miners started a small settlement at the landing which became Ste. Genevieve.

By the 1750's it had grown from a cluster of cabins into a prospering frontier village. Part of Ste. Genevieve's attraction was that it was situated on the edge of a rich alluvial floodplain that was ideal for farming. It soon became a shipping point not only for lead but for salt and a variety of agricultural products. Residents of this community cultivated a lifestyle unique to this valley building plantation homes and importing clothing and other items from their native France.

In 1785 Ste. Genevieve had nearly 800 inhabitants when it was struck by a devastating flood. The damage was so total that residents reluctantly agreed to relocate the town to a site on higher ground two miles upriver. Safe from flooding the new Ste. Genevieve grew at a brisk pace over the next two decades and in 1805 it had nearly 3,000 inhabitants.

Ste. Genevieve however, lacked the energy to sustain its growth. In the 1820's and 1830's its trading network was disrupted by the new towns that were springing up along the Mississippi and when the price of lead declined in the 1850's its economy stagnated. By 1860 this once prominent French settlement had faded into obscurity.

In spite of Ste. Genevieve's problems, there was enough residual wealth among the citizens to maintain and preserve the gracious French Colonial homes built by their ancestors. Modern Ste. Genevieve is home to nearly two dozen Eighteenth Century buildings and outwardly at least its downtown district looks much like it did in 1830. Of all the towns on the Upper Mississippi this is the one place that seems to belong to a different era and is close in appearance to a town of Colonial America.

Market St. looking East, Ste. Genevieve, Mo.

187
Guibourd-Valle House

Misidentified here as the Spanish Commandant's Home, this historic structure is one of a select number of Ste. Genevieve homes that date back to the Eighteenth Century. Now called the Guibourd-Valle House, its early history is shrouded in mystery. What is clear is that the house was built sometime around 1785 and its first owner was Jacques Guibourd who migrated from the Caribbean to Ste. Genevieve. The home possesses all the architectural features associated with French Colonial styling including a raised basement and a sloping roof that projects beyond the frame to form a cover for the porch.

The house was purchased in 1930 by Jules Valle who was the great, great grandson of the town's last commandant. Valle spent a fortune restoring the home and then furnished it with priceless European art objects. One of Ste. Genevieve's most celebrated house museums, the Guibourd-Valle House is located at Fourth and Merchant.

188
Ste. Genevieve Academy

This rather substantial building housed one of the first schools of the Upper Mississippi. Formal schooling was still very much a novelty, especially in the midwest when the town was granted a charter in 1807 to open a private academy. One year later work on this building was completed and in 1810 Ste. Genevieve Academy received its first student. Educating young women was still considered unnecessary so the academy was an all- boy school. The curriculum was tough and demanding with a strong emphasis placed on mathematics, Latin and Greek philosophy. Finding competent teachers was an almost insurmountable challenge and after years of struggling with this problem the academy closed its door in 1862.

Used for a variety of purposes and abandoned for long stretches of time, the old Ste. Genevieve Academy was reopened as a school for special education in the late 1950's. Vacated again in the late 1970's, this historic structure which is situated at the corner of 5th and Washington was recently converted into a private residence.

SPANISH COMMANDANTS HOME 1785
STE GENEVIEVE MO.

OLD ACADEMY, 1808, STE. GENEVIEVE, MO.

189
Price Brick Building

The building featured in this Ste. Genevieve scene, which for many years has been called the "Old Brick House," is the oldest surviving brick structure in the entire Upper Mississippi Valley. It was built sometime around 1790 as a private dwelling by John Price. A trading merchant, Price was one of the first Americans to settle in Ste. Genevieve. In the early part of the Nineteenth Century, this building was used as a courthouse and then in the 1830's it became a school building. Converted once again into a home sometime around the Civil War, this historic structure currently houses a restaurant.

Well over 200 years old, this building has managed to retain much of its historic integrity. It is situated at the corner of Third and Market.

190
Chester Cliff

Taken from a position about midway up the embankment at Chester, Illinois this photo documents two of the city's river-related landmarks or: the City Steps and the Cliff House. In 1880 the city built this stairway to forge a direct link between the town itself and its levee. Apparently people back then were more physically fit than we are today! The City Steps, a curious relic, is now a concrete stairway.

Built sometime around 1833, the Cliff House is one of the oldest structures in Chester. In the Nineteenth Century this building was a hotel that catered to rivermen and the legend is that Mark Twain was a frequent guest here. For most of this century the Cliff House, which offers an unexcelled view of the river, has been an apartment building.

CHESTER CLIFF, CHESTER, ILL.

191
Cole Milling Company

This impressive scene of the H.C. Cole milling plant at Chester, Illinois reminds us of a time in the Nineteenth Century when nearly every river town had a grain mill somewhere on its levee. Because flour was such an essential staple a community's first enterprise was usually its mill and this was usually built at or near the foot of the levee. This is what happened at Chester when in 1839, just after the town was established, Nathan Cole erected a mill on its levee. Under the management of his son, H.C. Cole, the mill operation deviated from the custom of selling only locally. By the 1850's most of the flour was going to markets in the south. His descendants built upon that framework and they owned and operated it successfully until 1971.

The plant in this scene dated from 1883 and it was the company's third mill at this location. This structure burned to the ground in 1915 and it was replaced by a larger more modern mill which is now part of the corporate empire of Con Agra.

192
Wittenburg

Wittenburg, Missouri was battling for its very survival when this picture was taken during the Great Flood of 1903. The town is 25 miles upstream from Cape Girardeau, Missouri. In the winter of 1839 seven hundred German Lutherans from the province of Saxony decided to emigrate to America and form a new church. During the voyage one of the five ships they chartered sank in a storm and fifty-three people perished. Dispirited and nearly destitute when they reached St. Louis, they used what little money they had to purchase a large tract of land in Perry County, Missouri. Wittenburg was one of the six communities which they established in the spring of 1839. To their dismay they found the land poorly suited for farming and they considered abandoning this struggling colony. They managed to persevere and in 1847 laid the foundation for what would become the Lutheran Church Missouri Synod.

Wittenburg has been plagued by many problems, not the least of which is its susceptibility to flooding. It has always been sparsely settled and today it is little more than a name on a map.

H. C. COLE MILLING CO., THE HOME OF "OMEGA" FLOUR, CHESTER, ILLINOIS, ON THE MISSISSIPPI RIVER.

193 (140 u)
Tower Rock

This ominous looking rock is the fabled Tower Rock. Beguiling and yet potentially dangerous, it rises the west channel of the river near Wittenburg, Missouri. An erosional remnant, Tower Rock is a three-quarter acre slab of limestone that rises to a height of eighty feet. The object of endless speculation and wonder, it attracted considerable attention in the early decades of the Nineteenth Century as one of the featured subjects in a series of travel books.

Needless to say, one would be foolhardy to even think about landing a boat on this rock. The best and safest places for viewing this rock are at Wittenburg or across the river at Grand Tower, Illinois.

194 (140 l)
Cape Girardeau

The building situated at the far end of this street is the Common Pleas Courthouse, which has been a landmark of Cape Girardeau since the mid-Nineteenth Century. In 1805 the founder of the town, Louis Lorimier, donated a tract of land for a courthouse upon which was built a modest log structure. By 1850 the county had a pressing need for a new courthouse and in 1854 work was completed on this two-story gray brick edifice. To create more office space, wings were added to the north and west face of the building in 1889.

With its elongated columns and well proportioned tower the courthouse has a decidedly southern look. It is surrounded by a park which, among other things, has a noteworthy cast-iron fountain that dates from 1911. Beautifully sited on a hill overlooking the downtown business district, this public building is located at the intersection of Spanish and Themis.

Tower Rock near Murphysboro, Ill.

View on Themis Street, Cape Girardeau, Mo.

195
Cape Girardeau Levee

This scene, represents a fairly common occurrence in the days of Mark Twain when at the start of this century Cape Girardeau was one of the busiest ports of call on the Upper Mississippi River. Much of the success it enjoyed was a result of its location. The town is nearly midway between St. Louis and Memphis and it also is close to the mouth of the Ohio River. In this era most of the boats that delivered freight to Cape Girardeau were vessels owned by the Eagle Packet Company. The owner of this packet line, Captain Buck Leyhe, had such a fondness for this community that he christened three of his steamboats "Cape Girardeau."

In the waning days of this century, Cape Girardeau remains one of the busiest ports on the Mississippi and the town has a number of river-related businesses. The one thing that has changed is the face of the levee where in 1964 a floodwall was built near where these people are congregated.

196
St. Vincent's Catholic Church

St. Vincent's Catholic Church is one of the oldest and most revered landmarks in Cape Girardeau. Originally a mission church, St. Vincent's was formally organized as a parish in 1836 under the direction of Rev. John Odin. Two years later the parish built a stone church, which was leveled by a monstrous tornado which roared through this town in November of 1849. Almost immediately they set about the task of building this edifice, which was consecrated in 1853. Gothic in design, the completed church had a number of unique features, including an altar built on its own foundation and a circular staircase which connects the sacristy to an upstairs loft.

In the early 1950's as part of St. Vincent's centennial celebration it was extensively remodeled, and then in the 1980's several hundred thousand dollars was spent restoring the interior. The church doesn't look anywhere near its age. It is perched atop a hill overlooking the Mississippi at the corner of William and Main.

St. Vincent's Catholic Church, Cape Girardeau, Mo.

197 (141 u)
Southeast Missouri State University

This imposing structure, Academic Hall, played a paramount role in insuring the survival of the institution, known as Southeast Missouri State University. In 1873 the state legislature established this school at Cape Girardeau, originally called Southeast Missouri State Normal School, to prepare students for a career in teaching. Like most colleges of its era, the entire institution was housed in one building, a structure built in 1875. Such an arrangement could have dire consequences as the school discovered in 1902 when the building burned to the ground in a midnight fire. The school's fate was hanging by a thread as its administrators pleaded with the legislature to appropriate money for a new classroom building. After a long deliberation their request was finally granted and $200,000 was spent on the construction of this building, which was completed in 1906.

Academic Hall now houses the school's administrative offices. It is located at 900 Normal Avenue.

198
Cairo Levee

This remarkable photograph has an almost anachronistic quality as it merges the past with the future showing a Curtiss-Biplane in close proximity to a steamboat docked at the Cairo, Illinois levee. The plane, which was piloted by Hugh Robinson, was the featured attraction of Cairo's July 4th celebration in 1911. Back then, the 4th of July was something people looked forward to with far more reverence than we do today. Everyone dressed in their best "Sunday-go-to-meeting clothes" to participate in a day of patriotic fervor. Things began with several hours of speechmaking at the town square, which was followed by the highlight of the day, a huge parade down Main Street. Then came the obligatory trip to the cemetery where the war dead were honored in a solemn ceremony. And as in our own era, the day concluded with a fireworks display.

One marvels at how much our world has changed since 1911. Now, of course, these steamboats would be the main attraction at a 4th of July celebration.

Missouri State Normal, Cape Girardeau, Mo.

199
Cairo Custom House

The Cairo Custom House is a magnificent example of mid-Nineteenth Century public architecture. Designed by Alfred Millet, who was the supervising architect of the U.S. Treasury, it took three years to build this Cairo landmark, which was completed in 1872. This three-story stone structure is an eclectic blending of Renaissance and Romanesque style. The interior is beautifully decorated with black and white walnut wood and equally impressive is its marble and black slate flooring.

In the Nineteenth Century the first floor housed the town post office, the second floor the custom house, and the third floor a courtroom. Gradually the federal government relocated its offices to other sites and in 1942 they deeded the building to the City of Cairo. Today this building at the corner of Washington Avenue and Fifteenth Street houses a museum which contains, among other things, a desk U.S. Grant used while he was stationed in Cairo.

200
Hewer Statue (141 l)

The left half of this bizarre looking drinking fountain is a famous statue called the "Hewer". Sculpted by George Bernard, a noted turn of the century artist, this statue depicts a man cutting wood to shore up a floodwall. The Hewer was commissioned by Mrs. W.P. Halliday as a memorial to her husband Captain Halliday, a wealthy entrepreneur and one time river boat pilot. Exhibited at the 1904 World's Fair, this bronze statue was presented to the City of Cairo in 1906.

Back in the 1920's this drinking fountain was detached from the Hewer. The statue is now in a small park at the corner of 9th and Washington.